Contents

Materials

This book uses materials mainly in grey-blue, cold and warm green tones, and combines blue and soft red tones to create tiny treasures.

The monochrome off-white and skin-tone fabrics are made from soft Indian cotton in various colours, which can be found in the Tilda range. These are used for many of the projects, such as Quilted Father Christmas, the Christmas Stockings, the My Town Placemat and the figures.

The cotton wadding (batting) for the quilted models and fusible adhesive are available from Tilda's partner, Panduro Hobby and quilting shops.

Buttons, paper elements, ribbon and gift-wrap can also be found at from Panduro Hobby and quilting shops. Bag rings and hangers for the cardholders, as well as the pins and hearts, are also available from the Tilda range.

A large selection of Tilda products is also available from Tilda's partner and their retailers.

Get the latest news and ideas from Tilda at: www.tildasworld.com

Making stuffed figures

To make a template, transfer the pattern onto cardboard, either using tracing paper or by gluing a copy onto it. Carefully cut the template out using a pair of sharp pointed scissors.

Cut out a piece of fabric large enough for the piece(s) of the figure twice. Fold the fabric in two, right sides together, and press (iron) the fabric completely flat. Place the template onto the fabric and draw around it with a thin marker pen.

Do not cut out the parts of fabric before you sew.

Sew a small seam, using a 1.5cm (⅝in) stitch. Be careful of openings and follow the project instructions carefully. For figures with thin necks, sew an extra small seam on each side of the neck to strengthen it.

Cut out the pieces. Use small pointed scissors to cut about 4mm (⅛in) outside the seam. Cut out a small curve at the openings in the seam.

For figures with bases, sew around the pieces after cutting out, before turning them inside out. This is described in more detail in each of the project instructions. Cut small notches in the seam allowance where the seam curves in, keeping at least 1mm (¹⁄₁₆in) away from the seam. Turn the base inside out using a wooden stick. Pull the stick up from the inside of the seams and press the inside out pieces. Keep going until your piece matches the shape on the template and everything is properly turned inside out.

To turn thin legs and arms inside out, push the blunt end of a wooden stick (such as a flower stick or similar) towards the tip of the arm/leg, see figure A. Begin at the foot/hand and pull the leg/arm down over the stick, see figure B. Hold onto the foot/hand and pull downwards while holding on, so that the leg/arm is turned inside out, see figure C.

A   B   C

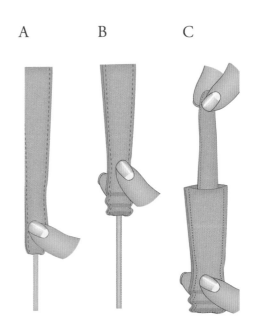

To stuff the head, start by stuffing the tips of the hair and nose. For the tips of the angels' hair we recommend rolling a lump of stuffing in your hand, pushing it into place with a thin stick and fastening a pin through the tip of the hair to keep it in place. You can use the same technique for small noses, such as pig snouts. Stuff the rest of the head.

To stuff the neck, avoid using two lumps of stuffing for a thin neck, as this will create a kink. Push a large lump of stuffing in with a larger stick and press it in until it fills the whole neck. If you do get a bend in the neck, twist a pointed stick into the doll. Hold the head straight and twist the stick up through the neck into the head. Break the stick off so it protrudes slightly from the bottom of the neck and leave it in place. This will keep the neck straight and not damage it. Do not use this technique for figures that will be given to small children. Stuff the rest of the body.

To stuff large simple shapes, first decide which is the right side and which is the wrong side. Place the stuffing loosely on what will be the right side, i.e. the side facing the room, for example, on a pig, and stuff towards the back. Press the stuffing well in towards the seams. Continue filling until the seams are as even as possible.

Place legs on angels, sew up the openings and attach the arms and ears as described in the project instructions.

If you find a bend or a bump on a figure, take a large pin or a long needle, stick it into the area next to it and use it to push the stuffing towards the bend or bump to even it out. This is also a good technique if the stuffing has worked its way out of a nose or similar so that it's too flat or dented. Use the needle to push the stuffing back inside the figure.

Painting on fabric

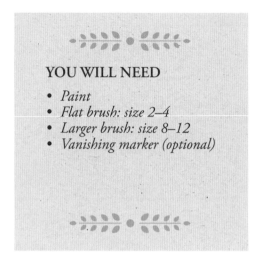

YOU WILL NEED

- *Paint*
- *Flat brush: size 2–4*
- *Larger brush: size 8–12*
- *Vanishing marker (optional)*

HAIR, TOPS, SLEEVES AND SHOES

The angels in the book have painted on details, such as hair, low-cut tops and shoes.

It is important to paint the pieces before sewing the angel together. However, the face should be painted (see Faces) after the figure has been sewn together to avoid smudging the paintwork while you are stitching.

Begin by drawing the outline of the hair, top, sleeve edges or shoes with a vanishing marker, using the photograph as a guide.

It is important to paint only one colour at a time and allow it to completely dry before starting with a new colour.

Generously load your brush then paint along the outline, keeping your edges as smooth as possible. The fabric absorbs some of the paint, so you may need to go over the lines several times. Next fill inside the outline. Lean the figure against glass or lay it on a piece of paper to dry.

Some colours cover better than others and you will probably need to use two or more coats of paint for lighter colours.

When all the pieces have dried, sew them together as described in the project instructions.

Faces

Stick two pins into the head to mark where the eyes will be placed. Remove the pins.

Use the eye tool from the Tilda face kit (ref. no. 713400) or the head of a small pin dipped in black paint to stamp the eyes where the pinholes are positioned.

Apply Tilda rouge, lipstick or similar with a dry brush to make the cheeks look rosy.

Appliqué

For the best results with appliqué, work slowly and carefully and don't worry about getting it perfect. Small imperfections are insignificant in the bigger picture.

The appliqué in this book was made using a good quality hand sewing thread in an off-white colour/ However, you can use colours that match the fabrics.

We recommend that you print the appliqué pattern out on a semi-gloss or gloss photo paper.

GETTING STARTED

Print out the project pattern and assemble it if necessary, so you have the whole of the model, complete with its appliqué.

Place the appliqué template under the wrong side of the fabric. In this book, we've used soft off-white cotton from the Tilda range. Draw both the outline of the model and the appliqué pattern lightly with a pencil.

It is a good idea to draw 2–3mm (⅛in) inside the pattern so that the appliqué easily covers the pencil line, see figure A.

A

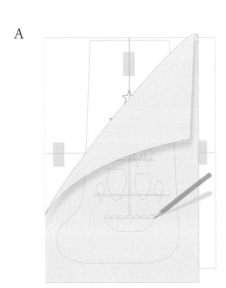

YOU WILL NEED

- *Fabric*
- *Glue stick*
- *Long, thin needle*
- *Hand sewing thread*
- *Pointed wooden stick*
- *Tweezers*
- *Semi-gloss/gloss photo paper*

CHRISTMAS STOCKING

The Stocking

Roughly cut out the stocking shape, preferably leaving a 5cm (2in) seam allowance, so you have plenty to work with.

The Owls

Cut out the appliqué pieces. The same shape can be used several times, but you will need both of the eyes, the tummy and the whole of the owl in shape in each size, as they are appliquéd in several layers.

Place the right side of the appliqué piece the against reverse side of the fabric and cut the fabric approximately 6mm (¼in) outside of the pattern piece.

Apply the glue stick around the edge of the template. Slowly press the fabric edge against the reverse side of the pattern piece so the fabric is glued firmly around the edge of the template. You can also apply glue to the fabric where this is easier.

When you come to an inward curve, cut one or two notches in the fabric to make it follow the template.

Use a small amount of glue to stick down any tips that have a point or a corner, see figure B.

Apply glue to the folded-in edge. Hold the appliqué in place against the background fabric while you sew around it. Use small stitches to be as invisible as possible, see figure C.

Snip the background fabric on the reverse side of the appliqué. Use the point of a wooden stick or your nails to loosen the glued edge away from the template. Ease out the template, see figure D.

Apply a little glue under the cut edges and press them against the appliqué so they stay in place. If you wish to appliqué several layers, such as on the Owls, continue in the same way on top of the first appliqué. Snip this as you cut the background fabric, to ease out the template.

B   C   D

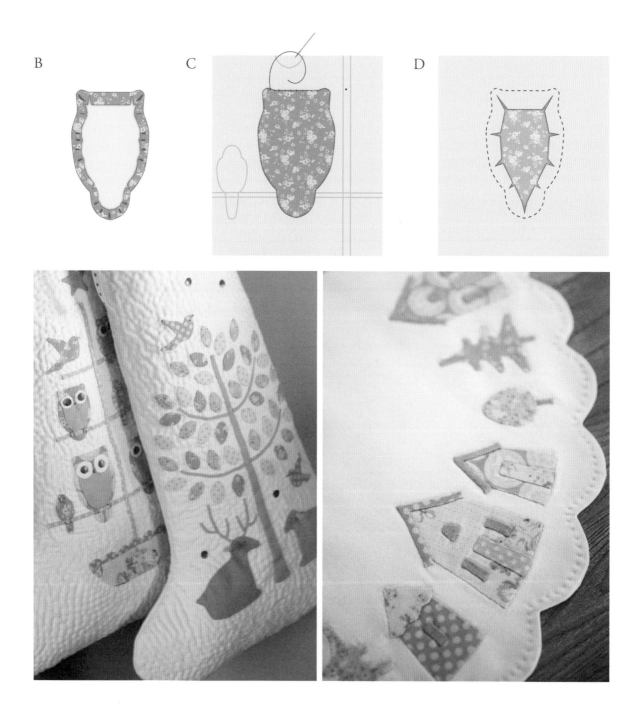

For smaller, more complicated shapes, such as the Christmas tree for the My town placemat and the berries and birds, it is a good idea to sew extra close stitches and use tweezers to remove the template.

Thin branches, tree trunks, antlers and windows are best made by cutting a strip of fabric measuring just over double the width of the strip you need. Apply glue along the length of the strip and fold/roll in the long sides so they stick.

Cut to the length of the pattern so you have a small tip at each end, which you sew in. Apply glue to the folded strip and place on the background fabric before sewing it in place.

Roofs and doors for small houses are also easier to fold with glue rather than using an appliqué template. Draw the roof on the reverse side of the fabric, cut so you have a folding edge all around. Cut a notch in the folding edge where the corner of the roof goes in, see figure E. Apply glue to the reverse side and secure in the edges before sewing the roof in place.

Press (iron) the reverse of the appliquéd fabric carefully so that all cutting edges face in towards the appliqué.

E

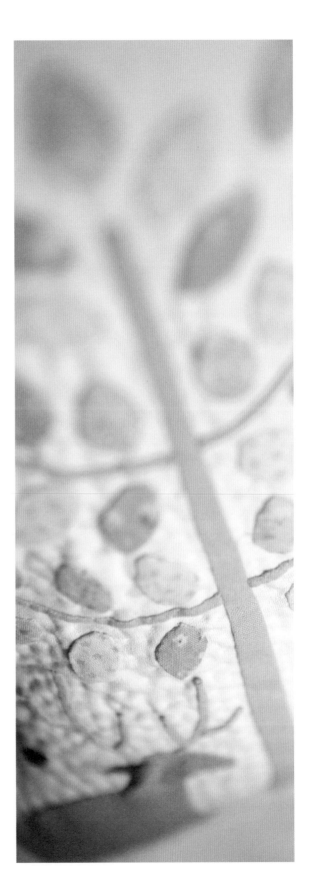

Assembling and hand quilting

Quilting by hand, like crocheting or knitting, is the perfect job to do when sitting on the sofa of an evening.

Spray glue (basting spray) is used to stick wadding (batting) and fabric together, making the task much easier. It is designed especially for this purpose and is available from quilting shops.

Quilting can hurt your fingers and damage cuticles; if you don't like thimbles, it can be a good idea to swap between a short and a longer needle to avoid this. We recommend starting with a thin, short needle for quilting.

GETTING STARTED

Make sure the front panel of the patchwork or appliqué is well pressed (ironed) and flat.

Cover your work surface with oilcloth, gift-wrap or similar.

Place a piece of wadding (batting) large enough to cover the front panel on the table. Cotton wadding (batting) has a front and reverse side; the right side is softer and on the wrong side you'll be able to feel some small knots.

Place the front panel on the appliqué or quilt with the reverse side on the wadding (batting).

Fold one half over the other and spray glue on the wadding (batting), see figure A. Fold back and smooth it with your hand to prevent creases, then continue with the other half.

Turn the wadding (batting) over with the front panel and stick the lining fabric panel in the same way.

Now you can quilt without worrying about anything moving. As you work, the glue will break down a little and the model will feel softer.

YOU WILL NEED

- *Cotton wadding (batting)*
- *Lining fabric*
- *Spray glue (basting spray)*
- *Short, thin needle*
- *Hand sewing thread*

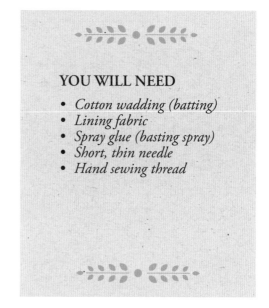

A

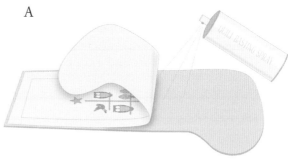

B

14

APPLIQUÉD MODELS

On some of the appliquéd models, we have added quilted dots that give an even structure and work well to emphasize the appliqué.

To do this, start by quilting all the way around the appliqué details. The stitches must be short on top and longer underneath. Here the quilting has a distance of 6–7mm (¼in) between the stitches, see figure B.

Next, fill out the areas between the details. Make sure the distance between the stitches is relatively even, both horizontally and vertically, so you get the impression of dots, not seams.

Continue to quilt a couple more circles around the whole of the appliqué.

Next, quilt along the drawn line around the whole model, so you can see where the pattern ends. It is worth going around a couple of times.

Finally, fill out the areas between where you have already quilted, stitching forwards and backwards between the shortest distances for best results. This is time-consuming but relaxing work that gives a lovely, slightly old-fashioned result.

When you finally reach the point of sewing the two pieces together, sew along the seam that was quilted around the whole of the model on the reverse side.

THROWS

Throws are easy to hand quilt, as long as you follow the line that joins the two fabrics.

It is slightly more difficult to hand quilt across a ragged throw. You will need to use a vanishing marker and a ruler, and draw a couple of crosses when you quilt.

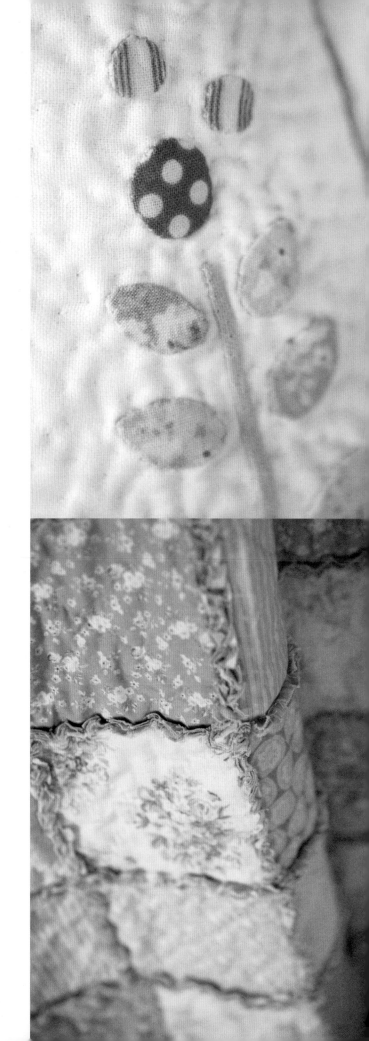

Welcome

A warm blue door decorated with spruce branches opens and a large hand quilted and appliquéd Father Christmas welcomes you.

A small fir tree is decorated with sewn stars in colours that match the door.

Come on in!

Quilted Father Christmas

This lovely appliquéd and hand quilted Father Christmas will take time to create, but it will be worth it for the delight it will bring to the family every year for generations to come.

If you want to make the design simpler, you can use fusible web for the appliqué details, instead of quilting. The jacket and trousers will then look slightly larger on the figure.

We recommend that you adjust the pattern depending on whether you use fusible web or wadding (batting) behind the fabric for the clothes.

You can find the templates in the Patterns section.

HOW TO MAKE

Body

Fold in half a piece of skin fabric large enough for the body, arms and legs twice. Press (iron) the fabric. Place the templates (see Patterns). Draw a body, two arms and two legs.

Sew around the pieces, paying attention to the position of the openings. The two openings for the base at the bottom of each

YOU WILL NEED

- Various fabrics
- Fusible web (optional)
- Wadding (batting)
- 6 assorted buttons
- Small loop or metal ring
- Glue stick and glue gun
- Long, thin needle
- Hand sewing thread
- Pointed wooden stick
- Tweezers
- Stuffing

side of the body must be open, although you will need to sew a small seam to hold the fabric together on each side of the base, see figure A. Cut out the pieces.

Fold the openings on the body in opposite ways so the seams are above and below each other. Sew a seam across each opening to make a base, see figure B.

A

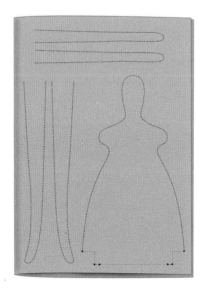

B

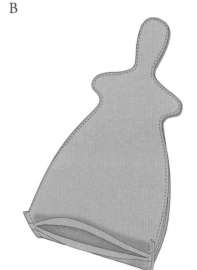

Turn the pieces fully inside out and press. Stuff the pieces (see Making stuffed figures).

Fold in the seam allowance around the opening at the top of the arms and stitch them in place at the shoulders. Fold in the seam allowance at the bottom of the body, place the legs in each side of the openings and stitch in place. To complete the doll, see figure C. The clothes will hide the stitches around the arms and legs.

Clothes

This Father Christmas is not designed to sit, but to hang against something. This means you only need to hand quilt the front of the jacket, trouser legs and hat. The sleeves must be quilted at the front and back as they are sewn from one piece and curved, so the wrong side comes forward.

Start by printing out and assembling the pattern for the jacket front (see Appliqué). Next print the pattern for the sleeves, trousers and hat.

Place the pattern for the jacket front under the freshly pressed fabric and draw the outline and all the pieces for the appliqué (see Appliqué). Repeat for the front of the hat, the four trouser pieces and two sleeves, where the curved edges are to be appliquéd.

Next draw and cut out the pieces for the reverse of the jacket and hat. Note that the reverse of the hat curves down; the front curves up.

Cut out the appliqué pieces. Identical shapes can generally be used several times, so you only need to cut out one sheet of each size.

Appliqué the front of the jacket (see Appliqué), and see figure D. On the sleeves and trouser legs, the appliquéd edge must be folded in at the bottom and sewn into the seam where the trouser legs and sleeves are sewn together. Allow for plenty of seam allowance on all sides.

Fold and glue just the curved edge around the template, and only sew the curved edge in place on the background fabric. Ease out the paper and sew a seam so that the seam allowances are held in place, see figure E. The thin dotted line marks the end of the pattern.

C

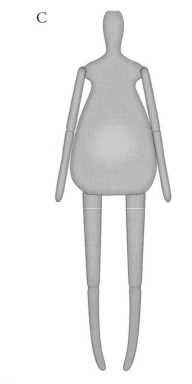

D

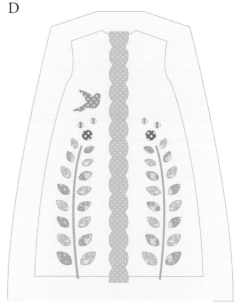

E

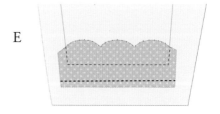

Assemble the front, wadding (batting) and reverse of each piece (see Appliqué). This is the same for the reverse of the jacket and hat, although they are not going to be appliquéd.

Altogether you should have two jacket pieces, two hat pieces, four trouser pieces and two sleeves assembled with wadding (batting), and a back piece, see figure F.

Quilt the jacket front, the front of the hat, the two opposite trouser pieces and the sleeves (see Assembling and hand quilting). Only quilt inside the drawn outline for each piece. You can also quilt the other pieces if you wish.

Once the necessary pieces are quilted, cut the seam allowances back to 1cm (⅜in) outside the pattern line so the pieces can be sewn together.

F

Jacket

Place the front and back pieces right sides together and sew the shoulders together. Fold the pieces away from each other and sew the sleeves in place, see figure G.

Fold the jacket right sides together. Sew each side and the sleeves together. Sew away from the side you have quilted and follow the seam you have quilted around the pattern piece, see figure H.

Trim off the seam allowance under the sleeves and trim down the seam allowance around the whole of the jacket to 5–6mm (¼in). Turn the jacket inside out.

Cut a long strip, 6cm (2¼in) in width, for the edging at the bottom of the jacket and press it in half with wrong sides together. Place the unsewn edge of the jacket against the other unsewn edge and sew approximately 1cm (⅜in) in from the edge, see figure I.

Fold the edge around the jacket edge and tack in place on the inside.

The neck opening can be edged by hand in the same way, this time with a narrower edge. Cut a 3cm (1¼in) wide strip, press it in half and tack it in place in the same way as the bottom edge of the jacket, approximately 5mm (¼in) in. Fold it around the neck opening and sew in place inside the jacket. The beard will hide the neck opening, so it is not entirely necessary.

Simply fold in and press the unsewn edge at the bottom of the sleeves. If you want to sew the edge in place it is easiest to turn the jacket inside out, fold the edge up and stitch in place before turning it back the right way.

G

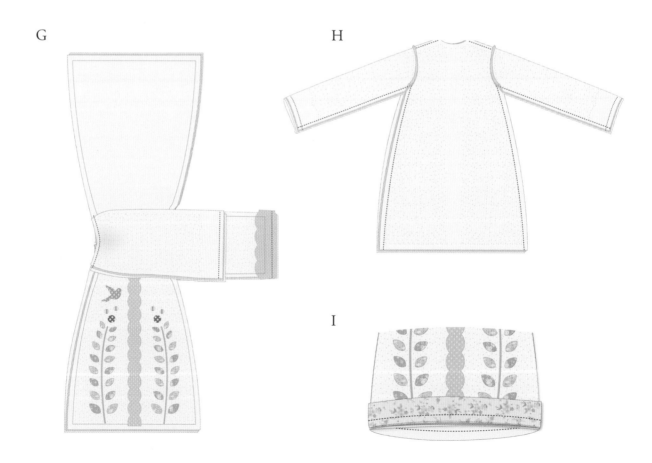

H

I

Trousers

Sew the two trouser pieces and two inverted trouser pieces together in the bodice, see figure J. If you have only quilted the two trouser pieces that are to be at the front, the two quilted pieces must be sewn together.

Fold the sewn together pieces away from each other, then sew up each side and between the legs, see figure K.

Trim back the seam allowance on each side and between the legs. Fold the seam allowance at the leg openings and tack in place while the trousers are inside out, see figure L.

Turn the trousers right sides out, press the bottom edge and pull them onto the figure. They must be slightly tight and do not need to be fastened. Do not fold down the edge at the top of the trousers.

Now dress Father Christmas in his jacket.

J   K

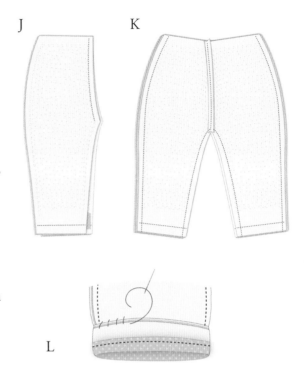

L
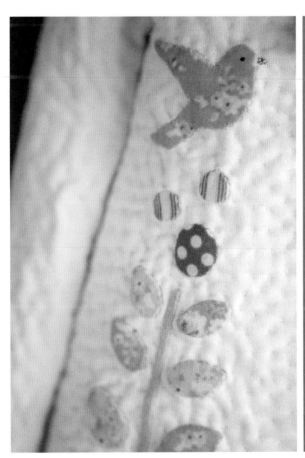

Hat

It is difficult to sew the edge of the hat neatly, as the hat is already sewn and the edge is more visible than the corresponding neck opening edge on the jacket. So, trim back the edge of the hat, cut a 3cm (1¼in) strip and sew the strip in place at the front of the hat using a sewing machine.

Keep a length on each side for the seam allowance so the edge doesn't get in the way when the hat is sewn together, see figure M.

Sew the two hat pieces together, fold the edge under so that it is not sewn into the seam on each side, see figure N.

Trim back the seam allowance and turn the hat the right way round using a wooden stick or similar. The rest of the edge must be sewn in place around the hat edge by hand, see figure O.

Then fold the edge around the hat edge and stitch in place, see figure P.

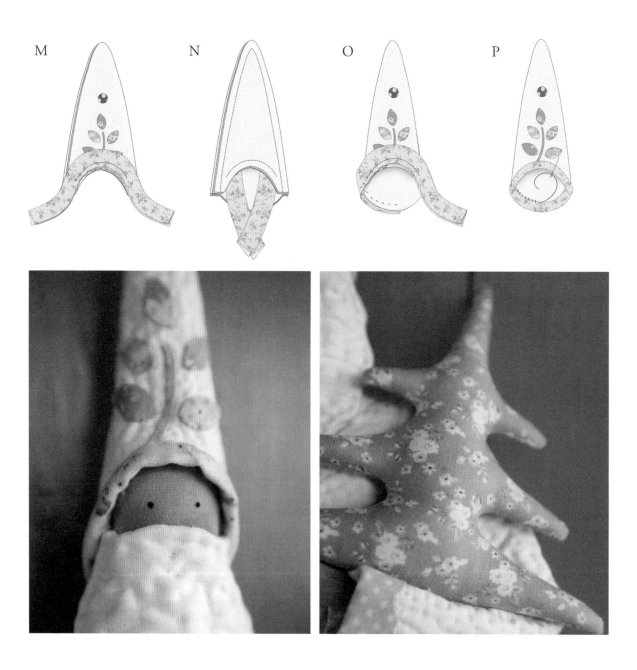

Beard

Press a piece of fabric large enough for the beard twice, right sides together, and place a piece of wadding (batting) underneath. Draw the beard and sew around, see figure Q.

Cut out the beard and cut notches in the seam allowance where the seams turn in between the curves.

Cut a reverse opening through one layer of the fabric and turn the beard fully inside out using a wooden stick or similar. Press the beard, see figure R.

Quilt the beard roughly, as indicated by the dotted lines in the pattern.

Attach the beard to the figure with pins and put on the hat. Use pins to determine the positioning of the eyes.

Remove the beard and hat again and make the face (see Faces).

Fasten the beard with pins again before stitching it in position, and then sew the hat in place.

Shoes

The shoes can be painted on at the end (see Painting on fabric).

Cut two strips of fabric for the edge of the shoes, approximately 3cm (1¼in) wide. Press in the edges on each long side so the strips are approximately 1.5cm (⅝in) wide and tack a strip in place around each of the legs so that the edge of the painted shoes is hidden.

Finishing touches

Sew the buttons onto the jacket.

Sew a small Christmas tree as described (see Christmas Trees), without a trunk. Fasten the Christmas tree and arm using pins, then secure in place with stitching or a glue gun.

Fasten a small loop or metal ring onto the back of the neck for hanging.

If the arm on the left side sticks out, or the legs jut out on each side due to the thickness of the clothes you can place a stitch between the sleeve and jacket itself, and between each trouser leg to hold the arm and legs in place.

Q

R
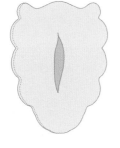

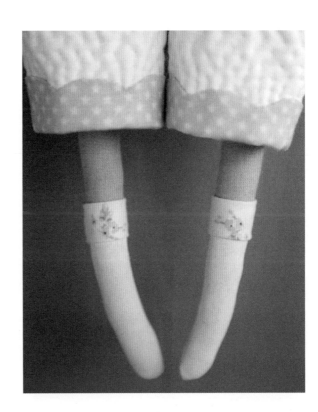

A cosy hearth

Family and friends gather around the living room fire, enjoying a well-earned rest.

Some of us chat, while others are busy crafting or reading a book. Full of hot, tasty cocoa and buns, we fall asleep on the sofa, surrounded by our loved ones.

Reindeer, sheep, owls, birds and a small forest of sewn trees provide the inspiration for the living room.

Hanging reindeer

Hanging reindeer are easy to sew as they only wear a torn off strip of fabric for a scarf. Their antlers are made from twigs, so be on the lookout for suitable twigs next time you're out for a walk.

YOU WILL NEED

- *Fabric for reindeer*
- *Fabric strip for scarves*
- *Skin-coloured embroidery thread*
- *Materials for face*
- *Stuffing*
- *Twigs for antlers*
- *Small loop or metal ring*

You can find the templates in the Patterns section.

HOW TO MAKE

Fold in half a piece of skin fabric large enough for the arms, legs and ears twice. Press (iron) the fabric. Make templates. Draw a body, two arms, two legs and two ears. Sew around the pieces, paying particular attention to the openings (see Making stuffed figures).

Bear in mind that the two openings for the base at the bottom of each side of the body must be open, although you will need to sew a small seam to hold the fabrics together on each side of the base, see figure A.

Sew all the way around the legs and arms. Cut out the pieces. Place a reverse opening on one layer of fabric at the top of the legs and arms, see figure B.

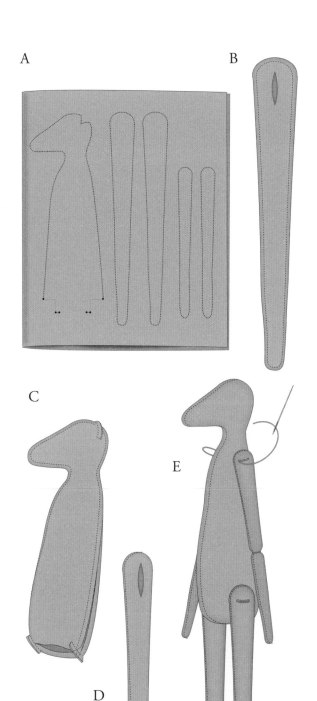

A

B

C

E

D

F

Fold the opening in the head the opposite way, so the seams lie above and below each other, then sew up the opening.

Fold the openings at the bottom of each side of the body in opposite ways and sew a seam across each opening to make a base, see figure C.

Stuff the body (see Making stuffed figures).

Stuff the arms and legs almost up to the dotted line marking on the pattern. Fix a pin across the arm/leg to hold the stuffing in place.

Tightly wind some sewing thread a few times around the arm/leg, tie the thread and cut the ends off, see figure D. Remove the pin and stuff the rest of the arm/leg.

Stitch the reverse openings. Attach the arms and legs by sewing across through the body and the arms/legs on each side, see figure E.

Bend the ears and sew them in place.

Make the face (see Faces).

For the scarf, tear off a strip in a fabric of your choice and fasten it around the neck.

Fasten a small loop or metal ring onto the back of the reindeer's neck for hanging.

Finally attach twigs as antlers. Twist some pointed scissors down into the head to make a hole for each antler. Cut off two equally-sized twigs, apply a little glue at the tips and twist them down into the holes.

These simple reindeer make cute winter decorations

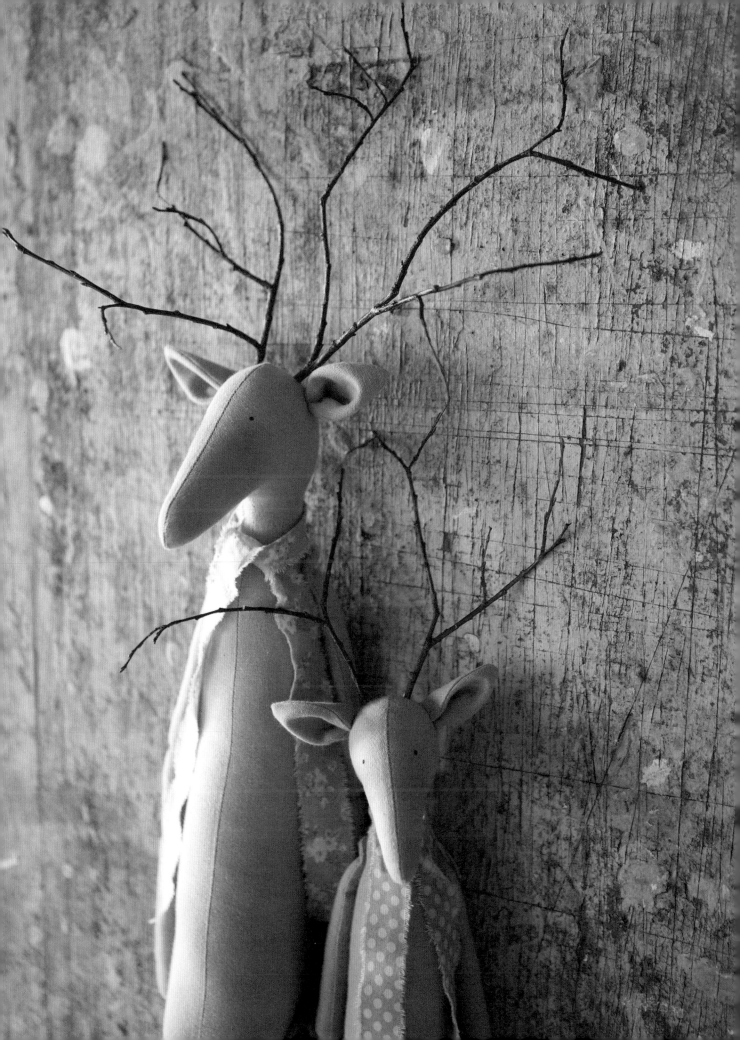

Christmas stockings

The Christmas stockings do not need to be quilted on both sides, as they normally hang with their decorated side facing outwards. However, you will need to assemble the fabric and wadding (batting) in the same way for the reverse as for the front.

For details on how to appliqué and assemble the layers and quilting, see Appliqué and Assembling and hand quilting.

You can find the templates in the Patterns section.

BIRDS IN A TREE APPLIQUÉ

Make sure that the perches are in front of the birds and behind the tree trunk and the tub when you appliqué.

The curved edge at the bottom of the tub is made by appliquéing one curve on top of another. Glue the fabric around the edge of the curve, but leave it open at the bottom. Sew along the curve, see figure A.

Ease out the templates and appliqué the tub above the open edges.

Owls

Fold in half a piece of fabric large enough for the owl twice and sew around it, see figure B.

Cut out the owl and turn it inside out. Fold the seam allowance in at the opening. Fold the owl and sew it in place.

RESTING TIME APPLIQUÉ

Make the thin reindeer antlers and branches on the tree (see Appliqué). It is easiest to roll the thin fabric strip up after the glue has been applied. Make sure the unsewn edges are underneath when you attach them to the background.

All the leaves are the same size, so the template can be used repeatedly. Here only two templates have been used to make the whole tree.

YOU WILL NEED

- Various fabrics
- Glue stick
- Hand sewing thread
- Stuffing
- Gold string or embroidery thread
- Gold or silver sequins
- Wadding (batting)
- Material for faces
- Lining fabric (optional)

Print out the templates, draw the pattern (see Making stuffed figures) and appliqué (see Appliqué).

A

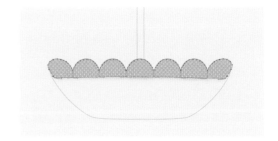

MAKING THE CHRISTMAS STOCKINGS

Assemble the pieces for the stocking with wadding (batting) and fabric (see Assembling and hand quilting). Note that the stocking pieces must be facing the opposite way to each other, see figure C.

Quilt just the front part, or both the front and back pieces (see Assembling and hand quilting).

Sewing the stockings

These Christmas stockings are not lined. If you wish them to be lined, sew a stocking shape out of lining fabric and push it down into the stocking before it is edged.

Trim the seam allowances to about 1cm (⅜in). Place the two stocking pieces right sides together. The reverse of the front piece must turn upwards. Sew the pieces together by following the quilted seam that marks the pattern edge.

Trim the seam allowance further and cut notches where the seam curves in. Sew a tight zigzag seam around the seam allowance to prevent it fraying.

Turn the stocking fully right side out.

Cut a strip of fabric 6cm (2¼in) wide without a seam allowance along the edge at the top of the stocking. Press (iron) the strip in half, wrong sides together.

Place the strip with the unsewn edge against the unsewn edge of the stocking and sew approximately 1cm (⅜in) from the edge, see figure D.

Fold the strip around the edge of the stocking and sew it in place on the reverse.

Cut a strip of fabric approximately 18 × 3cm (7 × 1¼in), adding a seam allowance. Press in the seam allowance, first along the short sides and then along the long sides. Then press the strip in half so it is approximately 1.5cm (⅝in) wide.

Sew up the open side. Fold the strip in half and stitch it firmly in place inside the stocking as a hanger, see figure E.

C

D

E

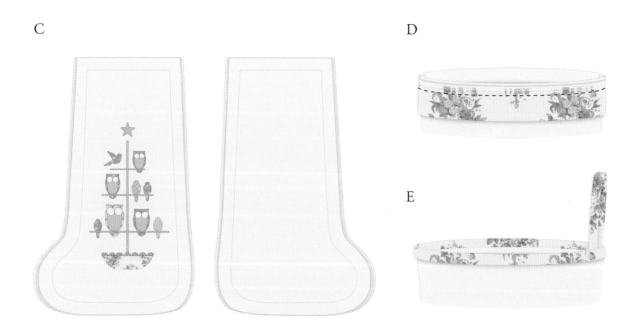

34

Faces

Make the faces of the reindeer and sheep (see Faces).

Paint black eyes for the birds. The owls' eyes are made using gold sequins, but you can use silver sequins if you prefer.

Beaks and claws

The owls' and birds' beaks and claws are made from Tilda gold string, but embroidery thread is a good alternative. The gold string is quite thick and you will need a needle with a large eye to thread it through.

Tie a knot at the end of the gold string and sew from the inside of the stocking. Sew a couple of stitches for each owl beak and one stitch for each bird beak and claw.

It can be difficult to pull a needle and string or embroidery thread through wadding (batting) and many layers of fabric. Try tweezers for better grip: use them to hold the needle when you pull the needle and string through the layers.

You can also sew on some randomly placed sequins or beads to decorate.

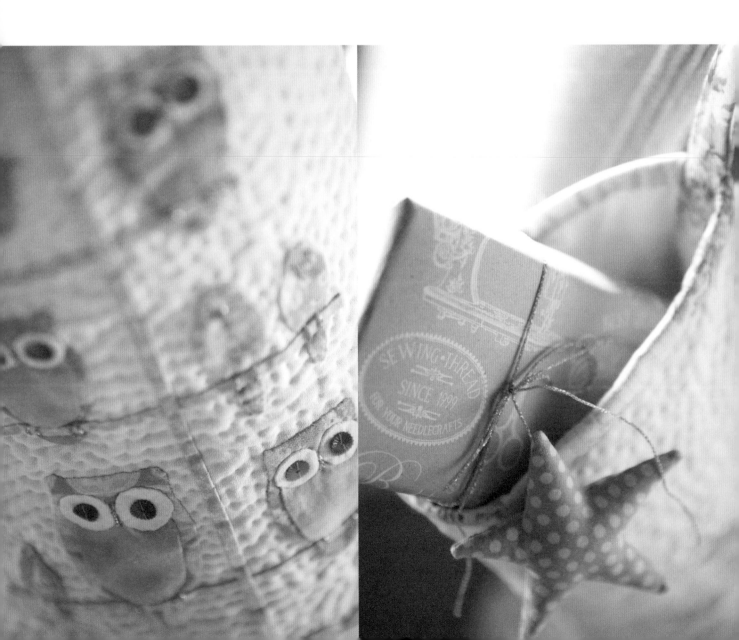

Owls

These small owl figures make cute Christmas tree decorations or are lovely as key ring toys. They can also be attached to a branch as a door decoration.

For smooth tummy and eye appliqués, glue the fabric in place with iron-on laminate film. This is quite stiff and a little rubbery compared to interfacing, so we suggest using a slightly thinner type, although most thicknesses will work. It is not suitable for appliqué on soft models, such as throws or Christmas stockings.

You can find the templates in the Patterns section.

HOW TO MAKE

Press (iron) a piece of fabric large enough for the owl's body twice, right sides together. Draw and sew around the whole body.

Cut out the owl's body and cut a reverse opening through one layer of the fabric, as marked on the pattern. The tummy and eyes will cover the reverse opening. Turn the body right sides out and press.

Stuff the body well (see Making stuffed figures) and sew up the reverse opening, see figure A.

Draw two eyes and a tummy on iron-on laminate film and carefully cut out without a seam allowance.

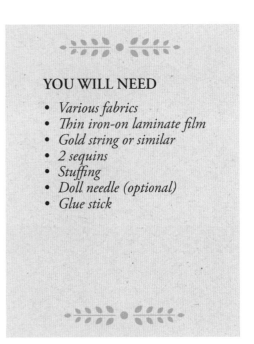

YOU WILL NEED

- Various fabrics
- Thin iron-on laminate film
- Gold string or similar
- 2 sequins
- Stuffing
- Doll needle (optional)
- Glue stick

A

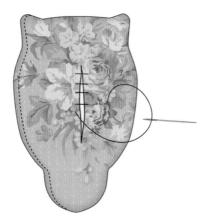

Hold the laminate film pieces against the desired fabric and cut the fabric so that you have a 6–7mm (¼in) wide seam allowance.

For small pieces it is easiest to glue the seam allowance in around the edges using the glue stick.

If you wish to press the edge in, place the laminate film piece on the fabric piece with the glue side up.

Use the tip of the iron and press the seam allowance in place against the glue side of the laminate film piece, see figure B.

B

Fasten the appliqué pieces to the body with pins so that they cover the reverse opening. The eyes must overlap the tummy.

Sew the eyes in place with small stitches around the edges and remove the pins.

If you use a doll needle, or a long needle, you can sew the loop, beak and claws with thread and avoid the problem of hiding knots.

Sew down where the loop is to be attached and come out again at the beak. Sew the beak, then the claws and come up again at the loop. Tie the ends of the thread together and you will have a loop for hanging.

Sew two sequins in place for eyes.

Christmas trees

Christmas trees in rustic plant pots make a great table decoration. The trees on their own will also make cute hanging Christmas decorations; simply fasten a loop to the top.

You can find the templates in the Patterns section.

HOW TO MAKE

Press (iron) a piece of fabric large enough for the tree twice, right sides together. Draw the tree and sew around, paying particular attention to the positioning of the reverse opening.

Cut out the tree and cut notches in the seam allowance where the seams turn in. Turn the tree inside out and press.

Stuff the tree well using a wooden stick or similar (see Making stuffed figures).

Twist a stick into the reverse opening and part the way into the tree. Sew the reverse opening around the stick.

YOU WILL NEED

- *Fabric for trees*
- *Stuffing*
- *Sticks*
- *Pot or cup*
- *Oasis*
- *Decorative sand, moss or similar*

Place the tree in a pot with oasis, then cover the oasis with some decorative sand, moss or similar.

Ragged throw

A soft throw makes you feel warm and cosy. I've been told that small children love these throws because they're fun to put on and they can play with the ragged edging.

The quickest way to quilt the throw is by using a sewing machine. A hand quilted throw has a softer appearance but is more time-consuming to make.

This throw is approximately 1.2m (48in) wide and 1.75m (69in) long.

Each made-up square measures approximately 13.5 × 13.5cm (5¼ × 5¼in), as they shrink a little when hand quilting and washing, in addition to the seam allowance.

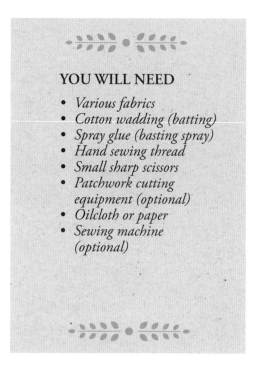

YOU WILL NEED

- *Various fabrics*
- *Cotton wadding (batting)*
- *Spray glue (basting spray)*
- *Hand sewing thread*
- *Small sharp scissors*
- *Patchwork cutting equipment (optional)*
- *Oilcloth or paper*
- *Sewing machine (optional)*

A

HOW TO MAKE

Preparing the patches

To make a throw like this one you will need:

- 117 squares measuring 16 × 16cm (6¼ × 6¼in) for the front.
- 117 squares measuring 16 × 16cm (6¼ × 6¼in) for the back.
- 117 wadding (batting) squares measuring 13.5 × 13.5cm (5¼ × 5¼in).
- Seam allowance is included.

We recommend that you use patchwork cutting equipment when cutting the patches and wadding (batting).

It is easiest to use the same fabric for all the patches on the back of the throw; we used a sand coloured fabric. The fabric you choose for the backing will also affect the front.

Plan the design on the front of the throw by laying the cut patches out on a table, see figure A. It is useful to take a photograph of the plan to refer to while you make the throw.

Cover your table or work surface with oilcloth or paper. Place a patch for the front of the throw with the right side down on the table.

Use the spray glue (basting spray) (see Assembling and hand quilting) to apply a spot of glue on the fabric patch. Place a square of wadding (batting) in the centre, so that it sticks to the fabric. Note that the wadding (batting) has a front and a back. The front feels softer and should face the fabric, see figure B.

Spray glue on the back of the wadding (batting). Place a square on the wrong side of the fabric, with the wrong side against the wadding (batting), see figure C.

You should now have a 'fabric sandwich', where the right sides of the fabrics are facing outwards and the wadding (batting) is in the middle. Continue until you have 117 fabric sandwiches.

If you wish to quilt by machine, sew across from corner to corner on each fabric sandwich before sewing the throw together. If you wish to hand quilt as here, quilt the throw after sewing the patches together, so you don't risk cutting the threads while sewing.

Sewing the throw

The seam allowance must face the front of the throw. This means that you place the patches wrong sides together (back to back) when sewing the throw together. Sew 1cm (⅜in) in from the edge, see figure D, stitching just outside the wadding (batting).

Continue to sew the patches so you have 13 strips with 9 patches in each strip.

When sewing the strips together, it helps to have the seam allowances facing the right way. If you place the strips on a table as they are going to be sewn together, the seam allowances on every other strip must be pressed to the right, while the rest are pressed to the left.

Place two strips wrong sides together, fasten a pin where the seams meet between each patch and sew the strips together, see figure E.
Sew all the strips together.

B

C

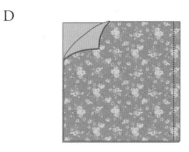

D

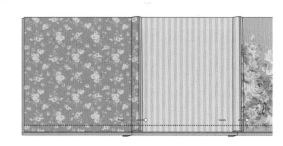

E

F

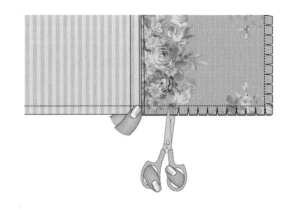

Sew a seam all the way around the throw to hold the layers together, 1cm (⅜in) in from the edge.

Sit on a comfortable chair and cut notches at 1cm (⅜in) intervals in all the seam allowances and also around the edges, see figure F. Make sure you cut both sides of the seam where the seam allowance is sewn in place.

Hand quilt the throw (see Assembling and hand quilting).

To machine wash the throw, place it in a closed duvet cover. It is a good idea to dry the throw in a tumble drier while it is still in the closed duvet cover.

Air the throw well before using.

Cushions

The cushions that pop up here and there in the book are very easy to make. To make the front more structured, the cushions are stuffed and quilted, then washed and tumble-dried.

Attach the stuffing and the back piece to the front piece of the cushion cover using spray glue (basting spray), in the same way as other quilted models (see Assembling and hand quilting).

Quilt the seams by machine or hand, following the pattern in the fabric.

Place the quilted piece, right sides together, with an equivalent piece of fabric for the back. Sew around, leaving a large enough opening in the base to stuff the cushion.

Turn right sides out, wash and tumble-dry the cover. Stuff the cushion then sew up the reverse opening.

A warm fireplace is extra cosy with homemade throws and cushions.

Toy animals

The inspiration for these animals on wheels came from old toys, although with twig antlers and angel wings, they are more suitable as decorations.

If you want to make them for children to play with, remove the antlers and wings and ensure that you sew the pieces firmly together.

You can find the templates in the Patterns section.

HOW TO MAKE

The method is similar to that of the lamb and reindeer (see Christmas Stockings). Press (iron) a piece of fabric large enough for the body, two ears and one tail, right sides together.

Draw and sew around the pieces, paying particular attention to the openings. Bear in mind also that the two openings for the base at the bottom of each side of the body must be left open, although you will need to sew a small seam to hold the fabrics together on each side of the base, see figure A. Cut out the pieces.

Fold the openings at the bottom of each side of the body in opposite ways so that the seams are above and below each other.

Sew a seam across each opening so you get a base, see figure B.

YOU WILL NEED

- *Various fabrics*
- *Cotton wadding (batting)*
- *Spray glue (basting spray)*
- *Hand sewing thread*
- *Small, sharp pointed scissors*
- *Patchwork cutting equipment (optional)*
- *Buttons for wheels*
- *Tilda gold wings (optional)*
- *Twigs for antlers (optional)*
- *Glue gun (optional)*
- *String (optional)*

Turn the pieces fully inside out and press. Fold and press in the reverse openings.

Stuff the body well (see Making stuffed figures). Sew up the reverse opening in the base.

Bend the ears and tail slightly, fasten with pins roughly, as shown in the photograph, and sew in place.

A

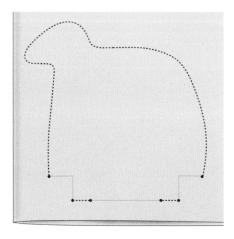

B

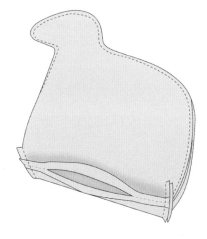

51

Make the face (see Faces).

Use pins to fasten four buttons onto the figure as wheels, making sure that it stands well. Stitch in place, see figure C. We have used wooden buttons, but fabric buttons are also cute if you want to add a little colour.

Gold wings are available from the Tilda range. For best results, attach these using a glue gun. Before securing the wings, bend them slightly so they stand up, as shown in the photograph.

C

Twist the tip of some pointed scissors into the reindeer's head to make holes for the antlers. Apply a little glue to the twigs before pushing them into the holes.

The animals are also cute with string tied around their necks to pull along.

Heart of a home

The kitchen is the heart of the home, where good food and sweet cakes are made. In the lead up to Christmas, the kitchen will be bursting at the seams.

Rose-painted pigs, hearts and a homemade angel watching over friends and family will add warmth, charm and jollity to the inviting atmosphere.

Rose-painted pigs

The pig's body is sewn in a similar way to that of the Toy animals. Although the shape is different, its base is sewn in the same way and the ears are attached as described below.

HOW TO MAKE

Tails

Cut a strip of fabric measuring approximately 1.5 × 7cm (⅝ × 2¾in) for the small pigs and 3 × 13cm (1¼ × 5in) for the large pigs.

Apply glue along the short sides of the fabric strip and fold in approximately 5mm (¼in) at each end. Also apply glue along the long sides of the fabric strip and fold in so that the edges meet in the middle.

Apply glue along one folded in long side. Place the steel wire in the centre of the strip with the curved side slightly inside one short side.

Fold the strip in half along the length so the steel wire sticks out the other side, see figure A.

You can find the templates in the Patterns section.

Sew up the short side where the wire doesn't protrude and the glued long side, see figure B.

Shape the tail into a curl. Twist the steel wire into the rear of the pig and stitch the tail in place with a couple of stitches, see figure C.

A

B

C

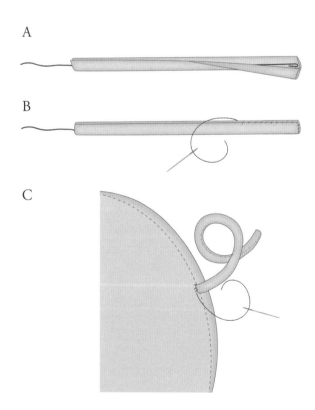

Roses

To make appliqué roses for the pigs you will need two similar fabric rose motifs.

Press (iron) a piece of iron-on laminate film large enough to cover the motif against the reverse side of one of the fabric roses. Cut out the motif; it is important to cut simple round shapes.

Pull the fabric from the laminate film, so that you have a piece of laminate film with the outline of the desired motif, see figure D.

Place the laminate film rose against the reverse side of the other rose motif. Make sure that the laminate film is placed in exactly the same place as it was on the previous fabric rose. Press the laminate film rose in place or use a spot of glue if there is no longer any glue on it.

Cut around the laminate film so you have a 6–7mm (¼in) seam allowance. Cut notches in the seam allowance where the curves turn in. Apply glue to the seam allowance a little at a time and press the seam allowance around the edges, see figure E.

Fasten the rose motif to the pig with a spot of glue and sew it in place using small stitches around the edges.

D

E

A delightful cake
ring stack with
small fabric hearts

Hearts

Hearts make ideal decorations for the heart of the home. They look especially lovely as decorations on cake stacks; a great alternative to sweets. Attach them with pins and use them again and again.

Hearts also make gorgeous Christmas tree decorations by simply attaching a hanging loop to the top. Or create cute garlands by sewing string through several hearts.

You can find the templates in the Patterns section.

HOW TO MAKE

Sew the hearts by pressing (ironing) a piece of fabric in half, right sides together, then drawing the pattern and sewing around. Leave a reverse opening in the seam.

Cut the heart out, turn it the right way round and press. Stuff and sew up the reverse opening (see Making stuffed figures).

The angel (see Homemade Angels) has light hair and clothes to match the kitchen. The seam along the edge of the jumper is sewn with red thread, and the paper rose is glued in place with an adhesive pad to make it stand out from the jumper.

party time

The dining room is decorated for a party, with festively dressed angels, an assortment of stars and romantic lit candles. The spruce garlands with cones reflect the welcoming forest outside.

In this section we also show you how to make a placemat appliquéd with small houses and trees that looks stunning as a table centrepiece.

Stars

The angels are the stars of the dining room with their pretty party dresses, but a sprinkling of stars will make the room look extra special. A mix of sewn, button and wooden stars and star-shaped tea lights will create a fabulous party atmosphere.

HOW TO MAKE

Sew the stars by pressing (ironing) a piece of fabric in half, right sides together, drawing the pattern and sewing around. Leave a reverse opening in the seam. Cut the star out, turn it right sides out and press. Stuff and sew up the reverse opening.

You can find the instructions for the angels in Sewing Angels. Here they have a painted sleeveless top decorated with sequins; otherwise, the instructions are the same.

A sprinkling
of stars

Angel busts

You can quickly sew a collection of these decorative angel busts. They are sewn in one piece and can be embellished in many ways.

These angels look sweet on the Christmas tree, or make several in a row for unique garlands. With lavender mixed into the stuffing, they make great gifts that smell amazing. You can hang one on a door with a message, such as the name of the person who lives there, or why not place an angel on top of a cake ring stack for a heavenly treat?

You can find the templates in the Patterns section.

HOW TO MAKE

Press (iron) a piece of fabric large enough for the angel twice, right sides together.

Draw the pattern and sew around. Don't forget that you will need to have a reverse opening in the base, see figure A.

Cut out the angel and cut notches in the seam allowance where the seam turns in.

Turn the angel right sides out using a wooden stick or similar (see Making stuffed figures) and press.

Stuff the angel, also using a wooden stick (see Making stuffed figures), then sew up the reverse opening.

YOU WILL NEED

- *Fabric for the skin*
- *Stuffing*
- *Paint*
- *Brush*
- *Tilda gold or feather wings*
- *Materials for faces*
- *Materials for decoration and hanging up*
- *Wooden stick*

A

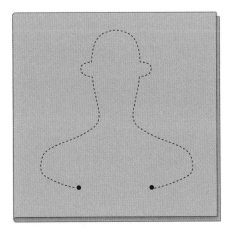

Paint the hair and top, then make the face (see Faces).

You can fasten some string in the top of the head to hang and display the angel.

Attach the wings with a glue gun. The gold wings are from the Tilda range, where you can also find feather wings that work just as well.

Decorate the angel if desired by sewing a row of sequins or beads along the edge of her bodice.

A small flower or bird made of paper can be attached with an adhesive pad so that it stands out from the bust.

If you want to make a garland of angels, sew the string through the top of each angel's head so they don't tip forwards.

A romantic detail on an old chest of drawers...

A choir of
angels on a
chandelier

My town placemat

Using appliqués of small houses and trees, you can create a miniature town around the edge of a placemat; the perfect centrepiece for a festive table.

The spruce trees are the most tricky to appliqué; replace these with round trees for a simpler design.

You can find the templates in the Patterns section.

HOW TO MAKE

Print, cut out and assemble the pattern, see figure A. Cut a 60cm (23½in) square strip of fabric. Press (iron) it in half, then fold it out again so that the folding edge marks the centre.

Place the pattern under the fabric and draw the outline of the appliqués and the curved edges (see Making stuffed figures).

Rotate the pattern by 180 degrees and draw on the other side of the folding edge, see figure B.

YOU WILL NEED

- *Various fabrics*
- *Background fabric*
- *Hand sewing thread*
- *Long thin needle*
- *Glue stick*
- *Wooden stick*

A

B

76

Sew a small stitch with darker thread between each of the curves so that you can draw the curved edge from the reverse side later. Sew down from the right side at the point between the curves and come up again on the right side, see figure C. Tie a knot on the right side and cut off the threads.

Cut out the appliqué pieces. Most pieces can be used several times and, since the large and small houses and simple trees are alike, you will need only one of each piece for these. The exception is the small spruce tree, where the shape is so complicated that the paper pattern can easily fall apart when it's removed. You do not need to cut out tree trunks, doors and windows.

C

Appliqué the placemat (see Appliqué).

Press the mat and place it on a table with the wrong side up. Position the curve pattern so you have a stitch on each side and draw the curve. Continue to draw one curve after another around the whole of the cloth, see figure D. Cut and remove the stitches between the curves.

The cloth is made of just two layers of fabric and does not need wadding (batting).

The back of the cloth is made of two pieces of fabric, so you will need a reverse opening.

D

Cut two pieces of fabric measuring approximately 30 × 60cm (12 × 24in), place right sides together and sew together, leaving an opening in the middle of the seam. Press the seam allowance on each side, see figure E.

E

Place the back piece and the appliquéd front piece right sides together, fasten with pins and sew around the curved edge.

Cut out the cloth and cut notches in the seam allowance between each curve.

Turn the cloth the right way round by pushing a wooden stick or similar into the inside of each curve and press well.

To make sure that the placemat keeps its shape when being washed or used, it is important to quilt one seam along the edge all the way around.

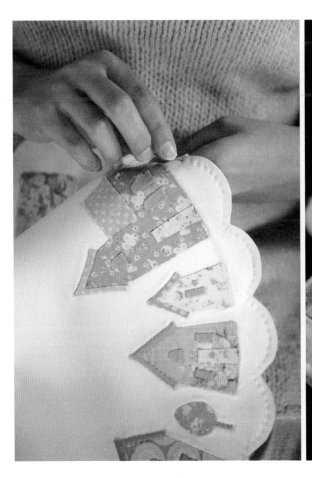

Sewing angels

There's a buzz and excitement in the Angel Workshop, where homemade angels chatter about skirts and discuss accessories...

Here you'll also find miniature sewing machines and cute patchwork pincushions in classic vintage cups.

Homemade angels

These angels have a charming homemade and naive appearance. With their thin legs and arms, and painted details, they are the Tilda version of primitive dolls.

The angel dolls can hold sewing equipment and could be given as a gift to a sewer or used as a decoration for the sewing room.

You can find the templates in the Patterns section.

HOW TO MAKE

Body

Press (iron) a piece of skin fabric large enough for a body, two legs and two arms twice, right side together. Draw all the pieces.

Sew around all the pieces. Keep in mind that the two openings for the base at the bottom of each side of the body must be open, although you will need to sew a small seam to hold the fabrics together on each side of the base, see figure A.

It is a good idea to sew an extra seam at the neck so that the seam is more robust when stuffing. Cut out the pieces and cut notches in the seam where it curves in.

YOU WILL NEED

- *Various fabrics*
- *Paint*
- *Brush*
- *Wooden stick*
- *Stuffing*
- *Tilda wings*
- *Materials for faces*
- *Glue gun (optional)*

Fold the openings at the bottom of each side of the body in opposite ways so that the seams are above and below each other. Sew a seam across each opening to make a base, see figure B.

A

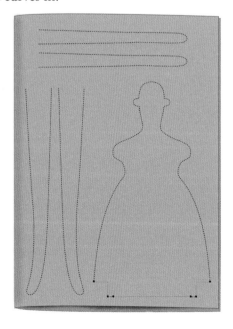

B

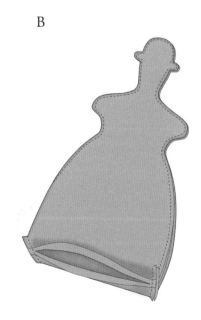

Turn the parts inside out using a wooden stick. Press all the pieces.

Stuff the pieces (see Making stuffed sigures). Use a wooden stick to stuff the legs and arms up to the dotted line on the pattern. Sew a seam across before stuffing the rest.

Fold the seam allowance in around the opening at the top of the arms and sew it up. The seam allowance at the openings to the legs should not be folded in. Instead, sew a seam where the seam allowance ends, so that the stuffing stays in place.

Paint on the hair, top and shoes (see Painting on fabric), see figure C.

Place the legs in on each side of the opening at the bottom of the body and stitch in place.

Bend the top of each arm around the curve on the shoulder and sew through the shoulder so that the arms stay in place, see figure D.

C

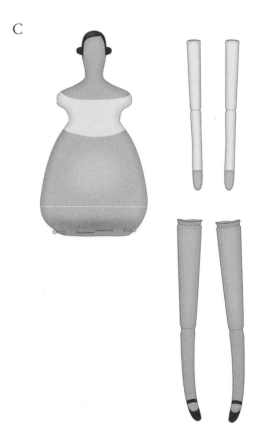

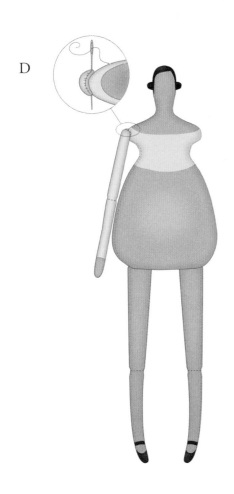

D

Skirt

Cut a 21 × 53cm (8¼ × 21¼in) piece of fabric for the skirt, adding plenty of seam allowance. Fold the fabric in half, right sides together, and sew up the open short side. Press in the seam allowance at the top and sew up the seam allowance at the bottom of the skirt. Turn the skirt right sides out and press.

Sew a row of gathering stitches at the top of the skirt. Position the skirt on the angel and pull the stitches to gather the skirt around the bodice.

Cut a strip of fabric for a belt measuring approximately 3 × 30cm (1¼ × 12in). Press in the edges along the long sides so that the strip is approximately 1.5cm (⅝in) wide. Tie it around the bodice, so that you partially hide the pleated edge at the top of the skirt. Fix the knot in place at the back with a couple of stitches so that it doesn't ride up, and cut off the ends of the strip at suitable lengths.

Make the face (see Faces). Glue or stitch the wings in place; the easiest way to attach them is by using a glue gun.

An angelic
line-up...

Sewn sewing machines

Small sewn sewing machines make a cute decoration for the sewing room, and the smallest version is the perfect accessory for homemade angels.

Small cotton reels are available in the Tilda range. The largest cotton reels are made from untreated wood and here they are coated with some slightly watered-down brown paint.

You can find the templates in the Patterns section.

HOW TO MAKE

The most challenging part of this project is sewing the machine in place onto the base, as it's a difficult angle for the needle. Stitching through the corrugated cardboard can make this easier.

On the large sewing machines, we have applied a coat of thin iron-on laminate film on the reverse side of the fabric to stiffen it. This isn't necessary on the small sewing machine.

YOU WILL NEED

- *Various fabrics*
- *Thin iron-on laminate film*
- *Corrugated cardboard*
- *Cotton reel*
- *Metal/plant wire*
- *Thread*
- *Hobby glue*
- *Paper flower or similar*

Press (iron) the fabric right sides together and draw the pattern. Sew around, leaving the opening in the base. Cut out the machine and cut notches in the seam allowance where the seams turn in.

Turn the machine right sides out and fold in the seam allowance at the opening, see figure A. Press the sewing machine then stuff well into all corners using a wooden stick or similar (see Making stuffed figures). Keep the opening in the base open.

A

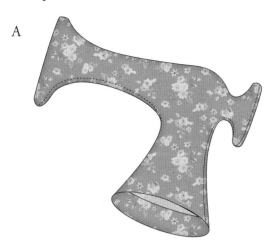

Sew yourself a
sewing machine

Base

The base should not be too light and thin, so use two layers of corrugated cardboard. Cut the pieces out according to the pattern and apply a little glue in each corner to stick them together.

Cover the base with fabric and stitch the edges of the fabric together underneath so it is stretched around the cardboard.

Place the sewing machine on the base and fasten with pins. The opening should be fastened in an oval shape on the base, see figure B.

Use a fairly strong needle and secure the sewing machine by stitching through the corrugated cardboard at the front, back and on each side. Tweezers can be used to pull the needle through the corrugated cardboard. Remove the pins.

Sew the edges in place between the stitches, using a smaller needle. Leave an edge open. Push the stuffing in through the opening between the sewing machine and the base until the it stands firm, see figure C. Sew the last edge in place.

Finishing touches

Cut three pieces of metal wire and make a small loop at the end of each piece. Apply glue to the

tip and twist one wire in as an attachment for the cotton reel. Secure the other two at the top and bottom of the front of the machine for the thread to pass through, see the photograph.

Wind the thread around the cotton reel and glue it over the metal wire at the back of the machine. Pass the thread through the other two loops. You can also add a small paper rose or similar to decorate (see Rose-painted Pigs).

B

C

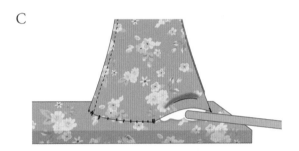

Patchwork pincushions

These are an ideal way to use antique cups or small bowls you have at home. Or visit a flea market and find a lone piece that deserves a new lease of life.

The quilting technique used is called 'English paper piecing', where you cover each piece of the pattern with fabric and sew the pieces together by hand to make a small patchwork.

You can find the templates in the Patterns section.

HOW TO MAKE

The pattern given here should be adapted to the cup or bowl you wish to use. Measure the diameter of your cup/bowl. The pattern size is calculated according to the dotted line slightly inside the pattern edge. The patterns given here are 10cm (4in) in diameter. If your bowl is 9.5cm (3¾in,) you will need to reduce the pattern to 95 per cent when copying it, and so on.

Print the pattern onto semi-gloss or gloss photo paper. Cut out the pieces, including the seam allowance outside the dotted line, see figure A.

The fabric pieces must be trimmed so they have a little more seam allowance than usual outside the paper shape, between 7–10mm (⁵⁄₁₆–⅜in) depending on their size.

Place the pattern pieces on the reverse side of the fabric on a hard surface. Apply a line of glue inside one edge of the piece of paper and fold in the edge of the fabric so that it sticks to it.

YOU WILL NEED

- *Various fabrics*
- *Thin iron-on laminate film*
- *Hand sewing thread*
- *Long thin needle*
- *Glue stick*
- *Semi-gloss/gloss photo paper*

Apply a line of glue to the next edge and the folded-in fabric and fold in the next edge.

Fold pointed corners as usual, allowing the corner to stick out, see figure B. When you later sew the pieces together, fold the corner on each side so you sew on the reverse side. Avoid getting glue on the folding edge.

The edges marked with a dotted line which marks the the seam allowance must not be folded in. Cut off along the edge of the paper, see figure C.

A
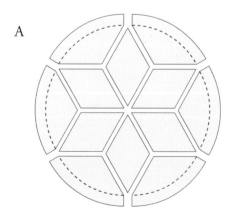

B
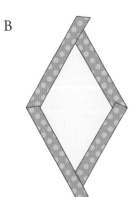

C
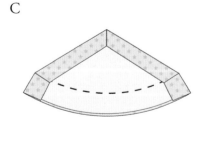

Place two finished pieces right sides together and sew the edges together with small stitches. This is so you only sew in the fabric and the paper can be easily removed. Continue with the next piece, see figure D.

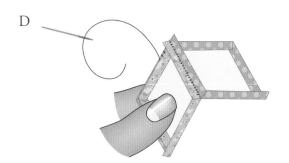

D

When the patchwork is finished, gently pull out the pattern pieces. Make sure the seam allowances lie inwards against the shape, as they did when the paper was inside. Press thin laminate film firmly onto the reverse side of the patchwork.

Cut a strip of fabric approximately 7cm (2¾in) wide, place it right sides together with the patchwork and sew it in place around the edge. Sew up the open side of the strip and cut away the excess fabric, see figure E.

The edge must be significantly lower than the bowl/cup so that the patchwork is not pushed up.

Fold in the edge if it is too high and stitch around the opening. Stuff the shape and pull the stitches to gather together, see figure F.
The opening should not be closed but adjusted so it fits well in the bowl/cup. Fasten the thread.

Place the patchwork 'cushion' in the bowl and apply glue to an area at the top of the edge a little at a time. Press against the cup/bowl edge until it sticks and continue with the next area.

It's difficult to get the edges completely even, but by gluing a little of the edge at a time, you will have more control. A little imperfection simply adds to the charm.

E

F

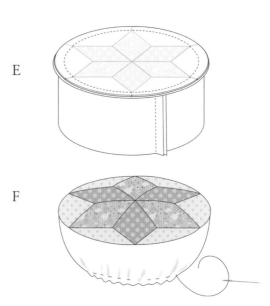

Cardholders

Your sewing materials need to be kept somewhere and it's good to be able to see what you've got. Materials that end up at the bottom of a drawer tend to be forgotten.

A cardholder can be used for many things by adjusting the size of the pockets. Here it has been made to hold Tilda button cards.

HOW TO MAKE

Cut a piece of fabric, a piece of wadding (batting) and a piece of backing fabric measuring 20 × 62cm (8 × 24½in).

Stick the pieces together using spray glue (basting spray) (see Assembling and hand quilting).

YOU WILL NEED

- *Fabric*
- *Backing fabric*
- *Wadding (batting)*
- *Spray glue (basting spray)*
- *Hand sewing thread*
- *Long thin needle*
- *Tilda bag clasp or metal hanger to fit*

When the pieces have been assembled, draw a rectangle measuring exactly 18 × 60cm (7 × 24in) and cut and trim the edges completely straight.

Cut two pieces of fabric measuring 4 × 18cm (1½ × 7in), and three pieces measuring 8 × 18cm (3½ × 7in) for the flaps. Add a seam allowance.

Iron the two narrower 4 × 18cm (1½ × 7in) strips in half, wrong sides together, so you have two 2 × 18cm (¾ × 7in) strips plus seam allowance, see figure A.

Fold the two wider 8 × 18 cm (3½ × 7in) strips, plus seam allowance, right sides together and sew up the open side, see figure B. Turn the strip right sides out and press (iron).

Measure 5cm (2in) down on the backing and mark right across with a line. Then measure 12.5cm (5in) down and mark. Continue measuring and marking until you have marked four sections of 12.5cm (5in) and a section of 5cm (2in) at the top and bottom, see figure C.

Place one narrow strip with the opening down so that the seam allowance overlaps the top line. Sew in place. The seam must be on the line and you should have 2cm (¾in) above the seam.

Sew the other narrow strip in place at the bottom in the same way, this time with the reverse opening facing up and 2cm (¾in) below the line.

Place the other three pieces in the middle of each line and sew in place with a seam in the middle so you have 2cm (¾in) above and below the seam, and the seam is on the line, see figure D.

Press the small flap at the top downwards and the one at the bottom upwards and fasten with a pin on each side. Cut away the seam allowance on the flaps so they are edge-to-edge with the backing. Fasten all flaps with a zigzag seam on each side.

Measure the middle of each flap and sew a vertical seam, see figure E.

Edge the cardholder in the same way as the Ragged Throw.

Fasten a Tilda bag clasp, metal clothes hanger or similar to the cardholder with a few stitches.

A

B

C

D

E

Sweet dreams

After a lovely day it's nice to go to bed with a good book and a well-behaved dog looking out for you.

In the bedroom you can find hanging lambs, purses and a simple-but-cosy throw sewn from fabric strips.

HOMEMADE

Purses

Small purses make great gifts for friends and are really useful for storing all sorts of items, such as coins, make-up and jewellery.

The pattern for these purses has been adapted to fit the Tilda bag clasp with light turquoise beads. If you wish to use a different clasp, the pattern will need to be adapted.

You can find the templates in the Patterns section.

HOW TO MAKE

Cut out a piece of fabric large enough to fit the purse twice. Draw the pattern on the wrong side of the fabric twice so that the bottoms meet, and then cut out, see figure A.

Appliquéd purses look best with wadding (batting); use normal fusible interfacing or thinner laminate film for plain purses. Cut out a piece of wadding (batting) or fusible interfacing in the same shape.

Attach the wadding (batting) by applying spray glue (basting spray) to the wrong side (see Assembling and hand quilting). Fusible interfacing usually has an adhesive side and is pressed (ironed) onto the wrong side of the fabric that will be on the inside of the purse.

If you want to appliqué the purse, draw the pattern for the details faintly in pencil on the right side and appliqué (see Appliqué).

A

YOU WILL NEED

- *Fabric for purse*
- *Lining fabric*
- *Wadding (batting), fusible interfacing or thin laminate film*
- *Spray glue (basting spray)*
- *Tilda bag clasp with turquoise beads*

Draw and cut out a corresponding purse pattern from lining fabric. On appliquéd purses, only quilt around the motif through the fabric and wadding (batting), as an extra layer of fabric would be too thick. Use the photograph to guide you.

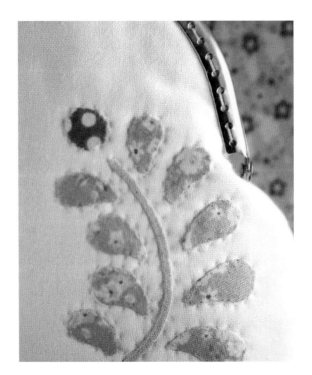

Place the fabric with wadding (batting) or fusible interfacing and lining right sides together and sew the curves together at the top and bottom. Note that a line on each side of the curve will show where the seam will start and stop, see figure B.

Fold the purse in the opposite way so that the folding edges are at the bottom and the curves stick out on each side. Sew up each side through the fabric and lining, leaving a reverse opening in the lining, see figure C.

Mark 2cm (¾in) up from the bottom of each side on both the fabric and lining. Fold so that the tip is flat and you can sew across, 2cm (¾in) in on each of the tips, see figure D.

Cut off the tips outside the seam and any unnecessary seam allowance around the whole of the purse. Turn the purse right sides out and press (iron). Sew up the reverse opening. Fasten each side of the curve with a stitch in the bottom hole on each side of the clasp to make it easier to hold in place while you sew.

Finally, sew the purse with double thread through the clasp along the whole of the curve and repeat for the other side, see figure E.

B

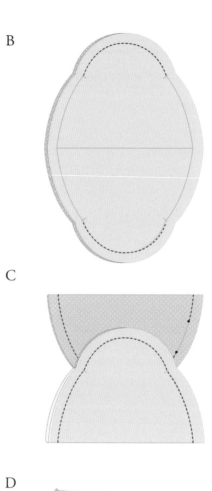

C

D

E

Hanging lambs

There can be no doubt that hanging these lambs with gold wings in the bedroom will bring sweet dreams… try it and see.

The lambs are similar to the Hanging Reindeer, although the pattern is slightly different.

You can find the templates in the Patterns section.

HOW TO MAKE

The pattern for the lamb comes in two sizes.

The body has a different pattern, but is sewn in the same way as for the reindeer (see Hanging Reindeer). The legs and arms are the same for the lamb and reindeer.

The lamb's ears are attached a little more to the side of the head and must be folded down slightly to give the appearance of lamb's ears.

Form a nose by sewing a long horizontal stitch across the pointed area. Then sew a long vertical stitch that will pull the horizontal stitch down to make a slack V shape, see figure A.

Attach the wings with a glue gun.

The lambs hold hearts (see Hearts). Attach these to the hand with a piece of string.

Make the face (see Faces).

YOU WILL NEED

- Fabric
- Skin-coloured embroidery thread
- Stuffing
- Tilda wings
- Glue gun
- Material for faces and heart
- Gold string or thread

A

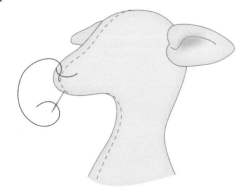

Strip throw

This small, versatile quilt is sewn from fabric strips. The quickest way to make these is to tear off strips from the whole of the fabric width.

This lap quilt is a great project for beginners, as you don't need a lot of experience at making seams.

HOW TO MAKE

The quilt measures approximately 1.1 × 1.7m (43 × 70in): the perfect size for children or to use as a lap quilt. It is very easy to sew, assembled from 17 strips measuring 10cm (4in) × the whole of the fabric width, see figure A.

If you want to make a wider throw, for the most attractive results it is best to sew three shorter strips together so you don't get a division between all the strips in the middle.

The pieces should be cut using patchwork cutting equipment to give you better control of the seam allowance in both directions.

Making a larger throw is more complicated and time-consuming. This patchwork assemble is made from strips measuring 10 × 50cm (4 × 20in), see figure B. It makes a finished

YOU WILL NEED

- *Fabric for strips*
- *Wadding (batting)*
- *Lining fabric*
- *Spray glue (basting spray)*
- *Embroidery thread*
- *Ribbon (optional)*
- *Patchwork cutting equipment (optional)*

throw measuring 2.2 × 1.5m (87 × 59in): a good size for a single bed. Seam allowance must be added to all of the above measurements.

A

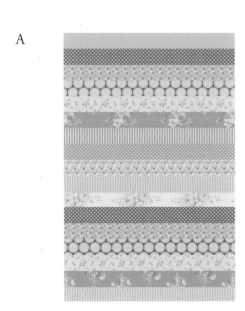

B

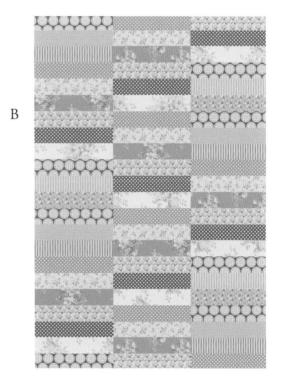

If you tear off strips, it is a good idea to calculate a 1cm (⅜in) seam allowance at the top and bottom to avoid having an unsewn edge.

Sew the strips together.

Stick the wadding (batting) and lining fabric together with spray glue (basting spray) (see Assembling and hand quilting). Trim the edges around the throw so they are straight.

This throw is hand quilted along the divisions between the fabrics after it has been edged. The thread is tensioned slightly along the way to create a wrinkly look.

The throw is washed carefully and dried flat. While it is wet you can even the edges around the throw and spread out the creases.

This technique gives the throw a slightly antique look. If you machine quilt, you must do this before you edge.

Cut 6cm (2½in) wide strips for the edge around the throw (seam allowance is included).

Join the strips together until you have a strip long enough to edge the entire throw.

Press (iron) the edging in half, wrong sides together, to make it 3cm (1¼in) wide.

Place the prepared strip with the open edge next to the edge of the throw and sew approximately 7mm (¼in) in, see figure C.

At each corner, fold in 7mm (¼in) from the edge and make a neat fold in the corner, make sure the strip follows the edge before continuing to sew, see figure D.

When you have sewn the strip in place around the entire throw, fold the edge on the throw under and sew the strip in place on the back, see figure E.

For a homemade finishing touch, sew on a piece of ribbon or make a personalized label.

C

D

E

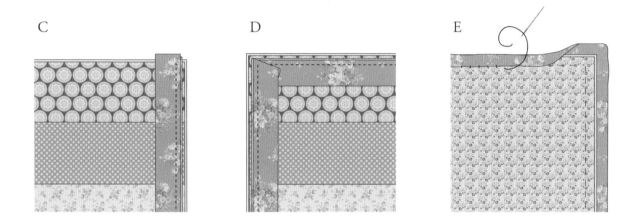

Acknowledgments

SØLVI DOS SANTOS
Our photographer Sølvi has worked with us on several Tilda books and always creates amazing photos. She has an eye for capturing designs and bringing models to life. Many thanks for the great pictures for this book!

INGRID SKAANSAR
Ingrid is a stylist and one of the main team members behind the projects. We wouldn't have managed without her. She keeps the whole project organized, and arranges and styles at an amazing speed. Thanks for your input!

TIRIL STENSGÅRD FINNANGER
A big thank you to Tiril, whom I'm really proud of for putting in a magnificent effort for this book. Whether he was holding ten rolls of fabric or a heavy tub of pigs, he always had a smile. It was wonderful to have him working with us!

TORJE NORÈN
My kind husband who took care of the heavy lifting, food and technical support as we photographed, while also doing his own job.

UNDHJEM MEDIA
Thanks to Tom Richard Undhjem for some excellent help.

CAPPELEN DAMM
Thanks to Cappelen Damm and everyone there who helped with the book.

Suppliers

EUROPE
Panduro Hobby
Järnyxegatan 17,
205 14 Malmö,
Sweden
www.pandurohobby.co.uk

Panduro Hobby
BP 500, 74305 Cluses Cedex,
France
www.tildafrance.com

Marienhoffgaarden
Industrivej 39,
8550 Ryomgaard,
Denmark
www.marienhoff.dk

STIM Italia Srl
Viale Carlo Troya, 7,
20144 Milano, Italy
www.stim-italia.com/shop/

UK
SewandSo
Unit 6A, Delta Drive,
Tewkesbury GL20 8HB
www.sewandso.co.uk

Threads and Patches
15 Watling Street,
Fenny Stratford,
Bletchley MK2 2BU
www.threadsandpatches.co.uk

The Fat Quarters
5 Choprell Road, Blackhall Mill,
Newcastle NE17 7TN
www.thefatquarters.co.uk

IRELAND
Puddle Crafts
33 Shop Street, Drogheda,
Co. Louth A92 KD50
www.puddlecrafts.co.uk

USA
Coats and Clark USA
PO Box 12229,
Greenville SC29612-0229
www.coatsandclark.com

Connecting Threads
13118 NE 4th Street,
Vancouver WA 98684
www.connectingthreads.com

eQuilter.com
5455 Spine Road, Suite E,
Boulder CO 80301
www.equilter.com

CANADA
Hamels Fabrics
5843 Lickman Road,
Chilliwack,
British Columbia V2R 4B5
www.hamelsfabrics.com

Patterns

All patterns are 100% size.

Seam allowance must be added to all pieces in the pattern unless stated otherwise in the instructions.

————————— An unbroken thick line marks seams and ordinary seam allowance where two pieces must be sewn together.

- - - - - - A thick dotted line marks openings.

- - - - - -
ES   ES = Extra Seam allowance. This marks openings where it is important to have extra seam allowance and where the seam allowance is sewn on each side by following the
- - - - - -   unbroken line. For example, at the bottom of trousers or at the top of a leg where the seam allowance will eventually be folded in or placed in the body.

A   Join   B   The joining edge marks the join between two pattern pieces, where the pattern is divided to make space on the page. The pieces for the pattern are joined together by the dotted line so that points A and A, and B and B, etc. lie next to each other.

Drawings with thinner unbroken lines are appliqués. Areas where appliqués overlap are marked with a dotted line. This means that you don't need to fold in the edge of the bottom appliqué, as it will be covered by an overlying appliqué.

- - - - - - A thinner dotted line marks knees, elbows, painted details and the bottom of purses.

See the individual project instructions for more detail.

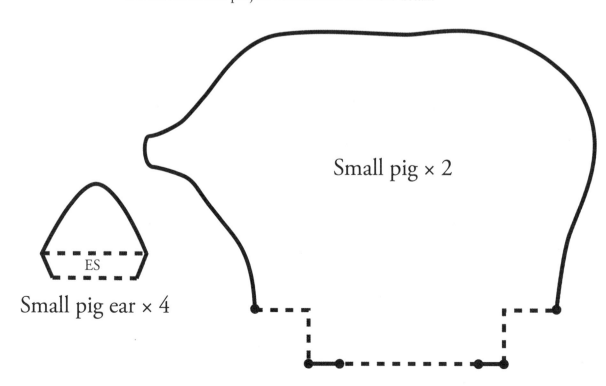

Small pig × 2

Small pig ear × 4

118

Rose-painted Pigs

Large pig

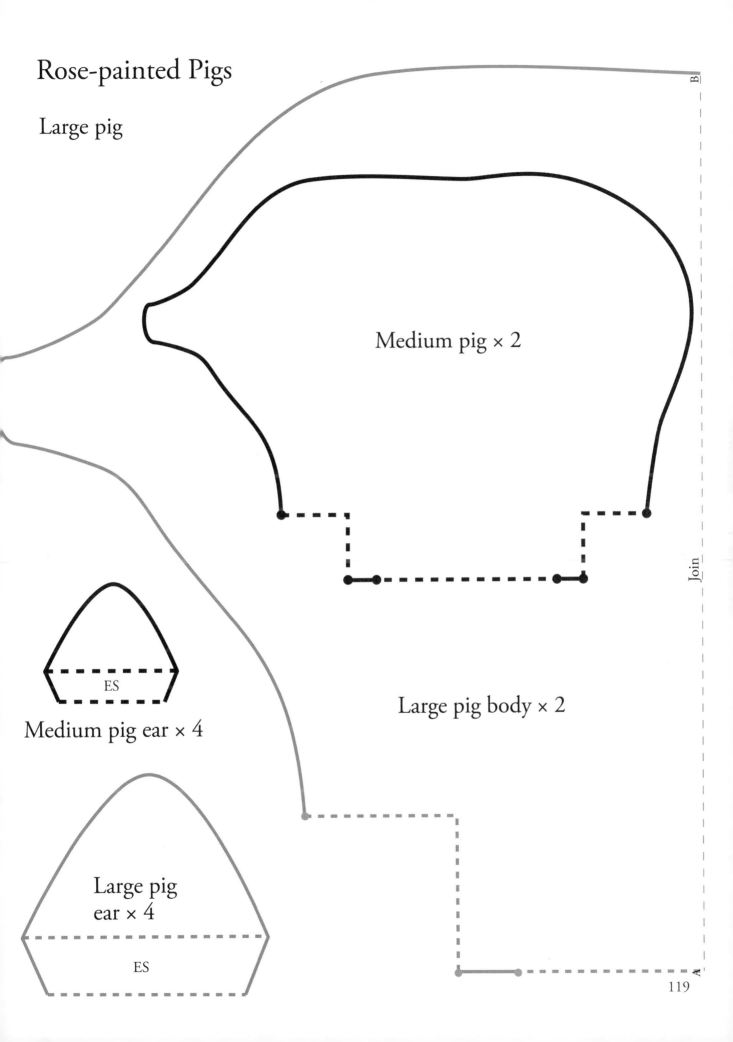

Medium pig × 2

Large pig body × 2

ES

Medium pig ear × 4

Large pig
ear × 4

ES

B

Join

A

119

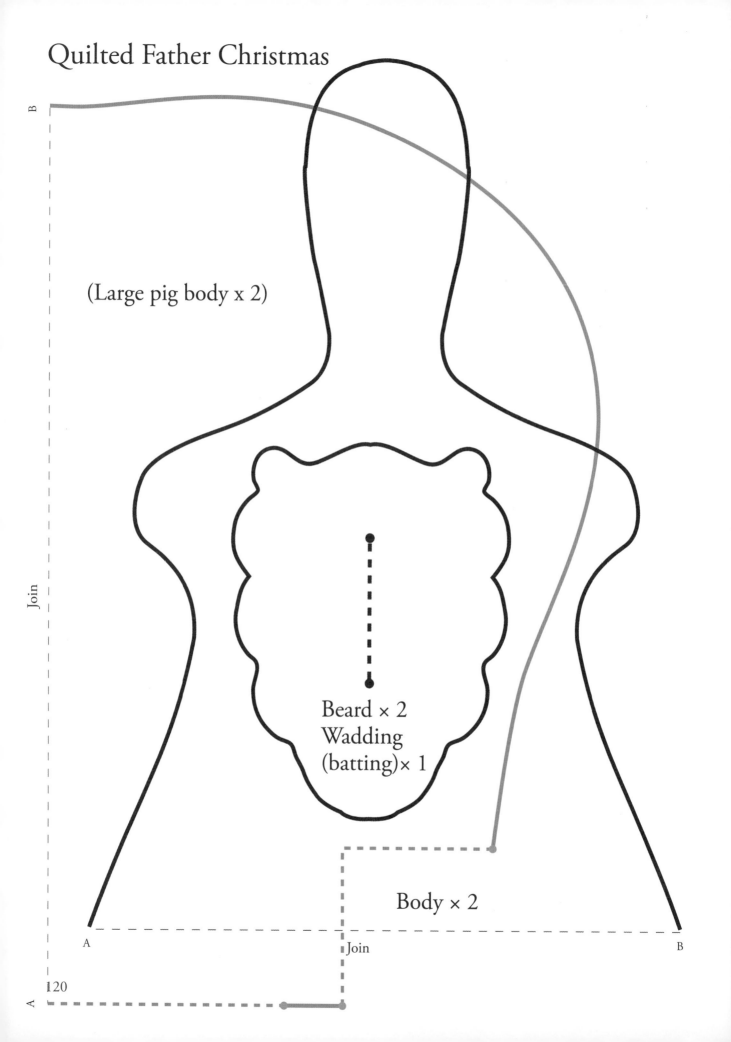

Quilted Father Christmas

(Large pig body x 2)

B

Join

A

120

A

Join

Beard × 2
Wadding
(batting)× 1

Body × 2

B

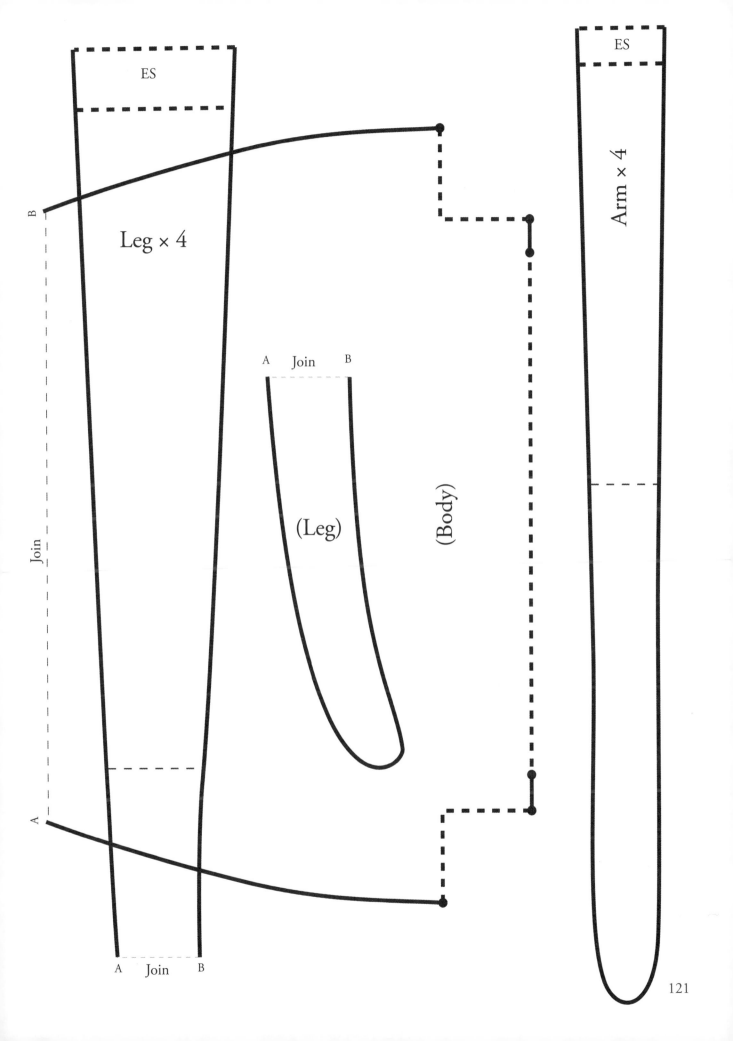

ES

Leg × 4

B

A

Join

A

A   Join   B

(Leg)

(Body)

A   Join   B

ES

Arm × 4

121

Quilted Father Christmas

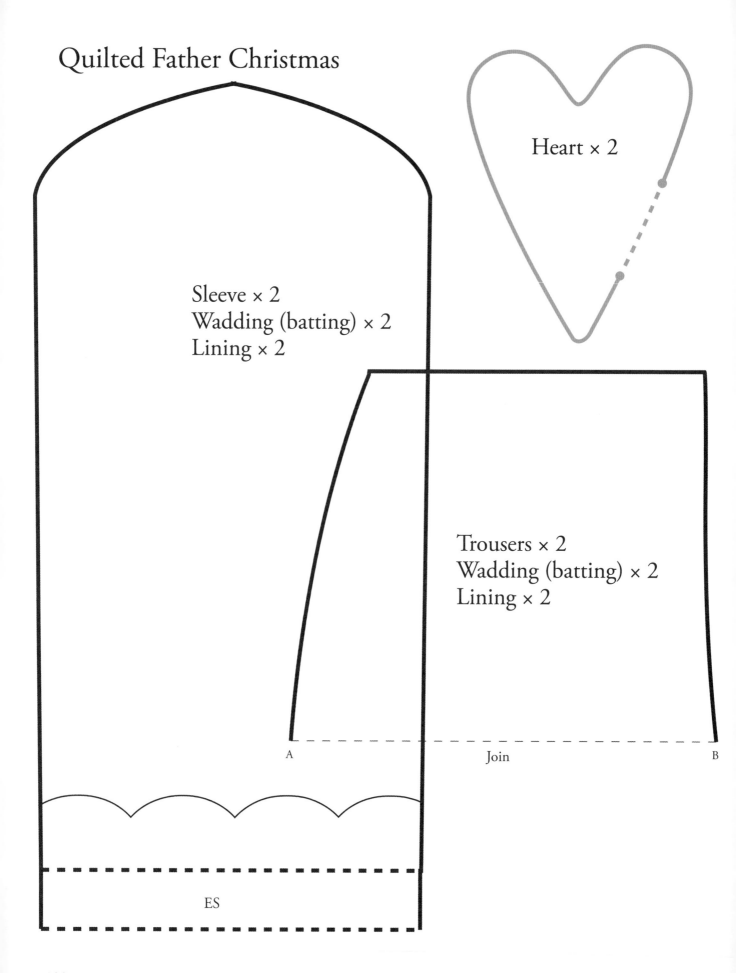

Heart × 2

Sleeve × 2
Wadding (batting) × 2
Lining × 2

Trousers × 2
Wadding (batting) × 2
Lining × 2

A   Join   B

ES

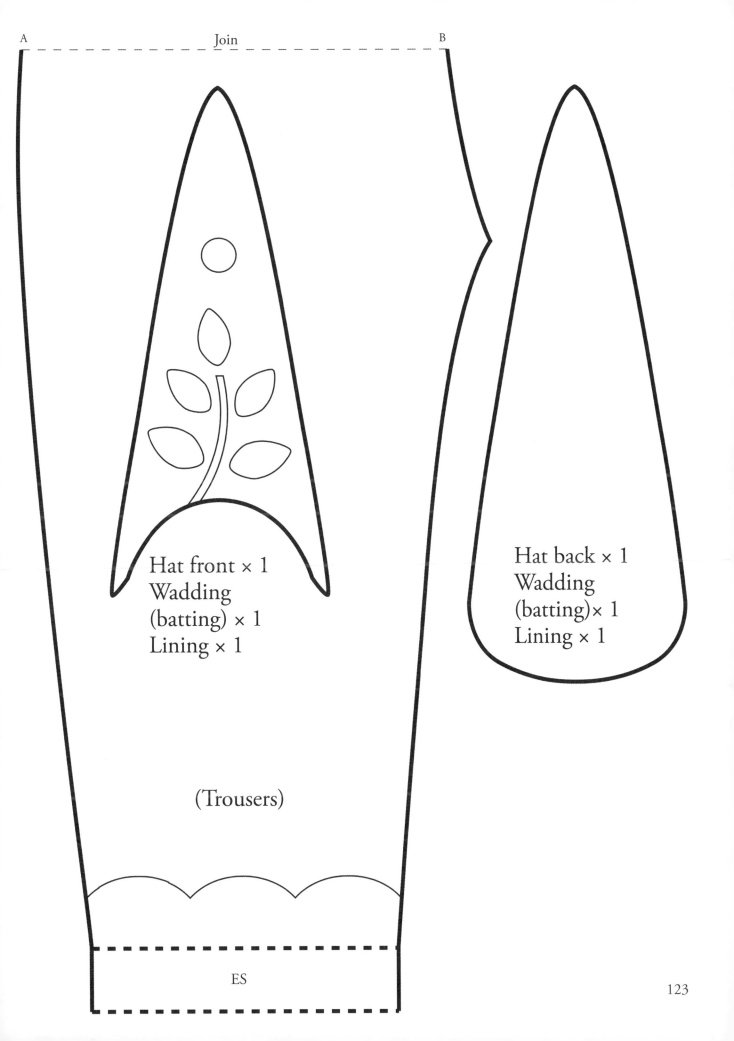

A   Join   B

Hat front × 1
Wadding
(batting) × 1
Lining × 1

Hat back × 1
Wadding
(batting)× 1
Lining × 1

(Trousers)

ES

123

Quilted Father Christmas

Jacket × 2
Wadding
(batting) × 2
Lining × 2

(Jacket)

125

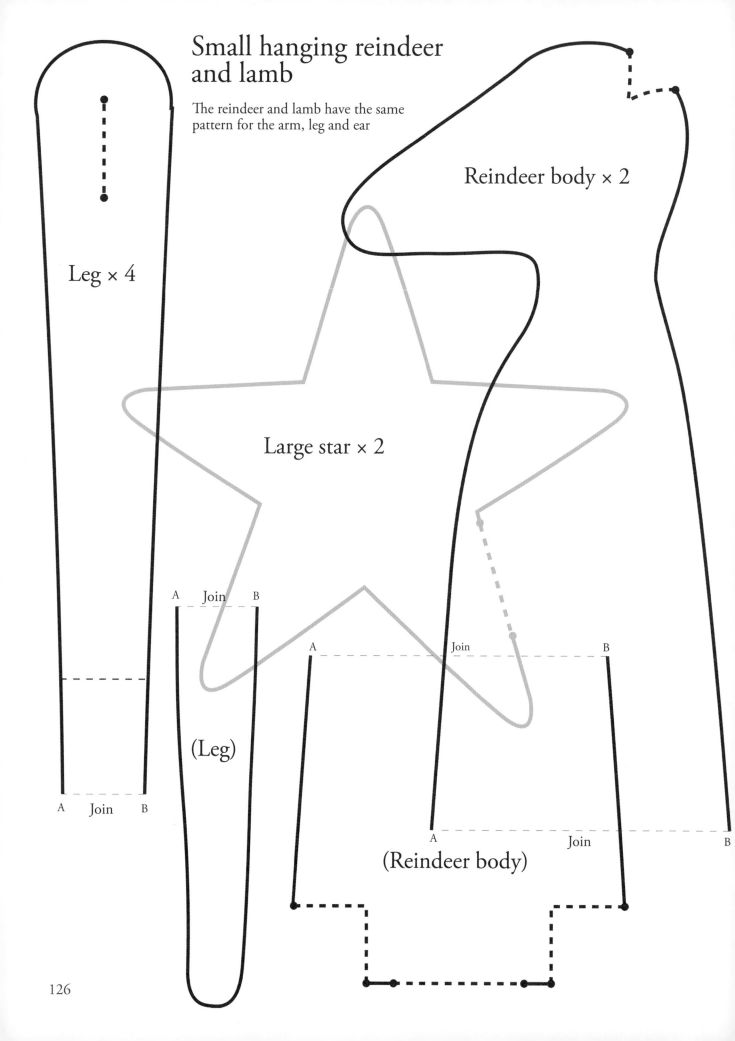

Small hanging reindeer and lamb

The reindeer and lamb have the same pattern for the arm, leg and ear

Reindeer body × 2

Leg × 4

Large star × 2

A   Join   B

(Leg)

A   Join   B

A   Join   B

A   Join   B

(Reindeer body)

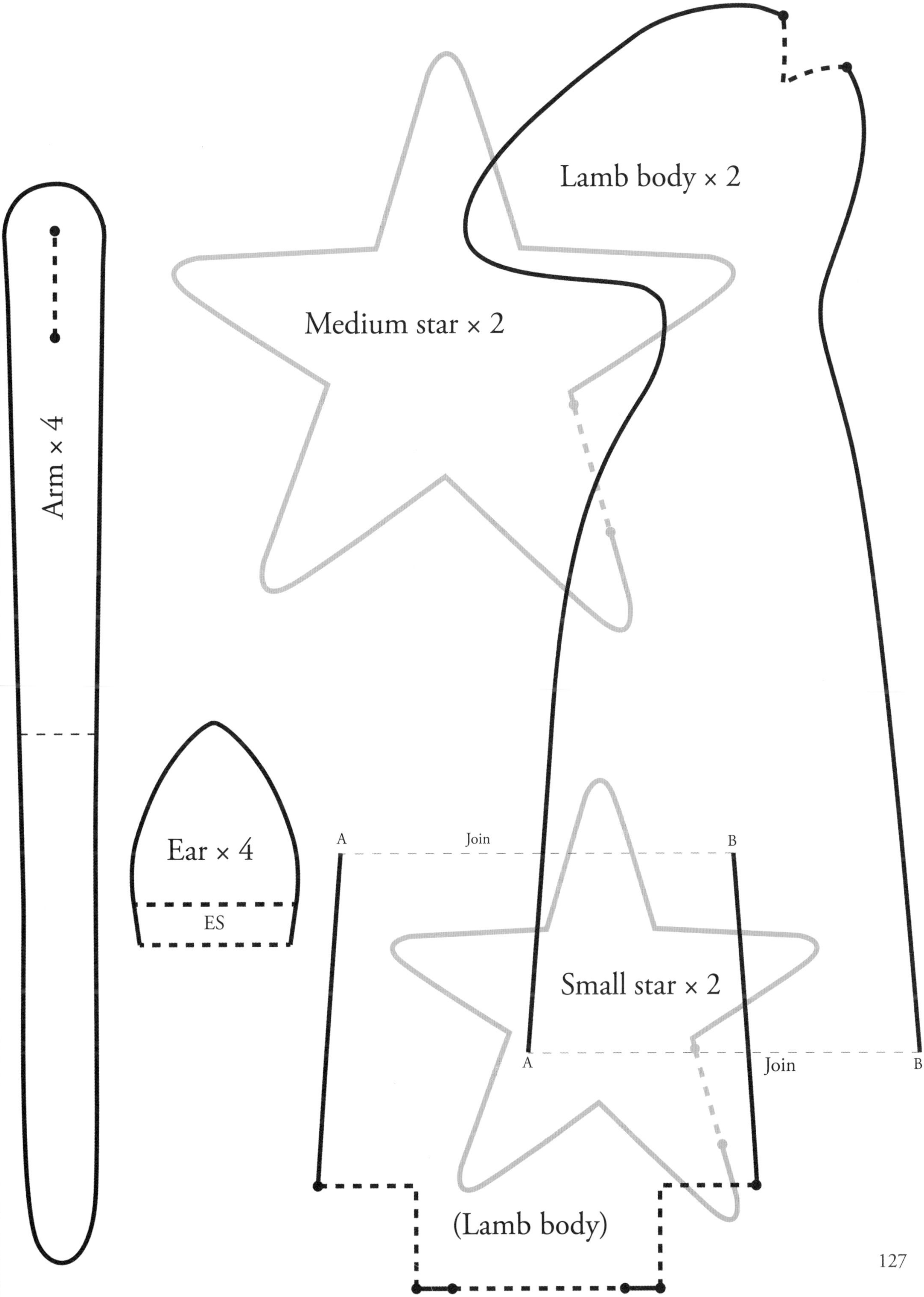

Arm × 4

Lamb body × 2

Medium star × 2

Ear × 4

ES

A   Join   B

Small star × 2

A   Join   B

(Lamb body)

127

Large hanging reindeer and lamb

The reindeer and lamb have the same pattern for the arm, leg and ear

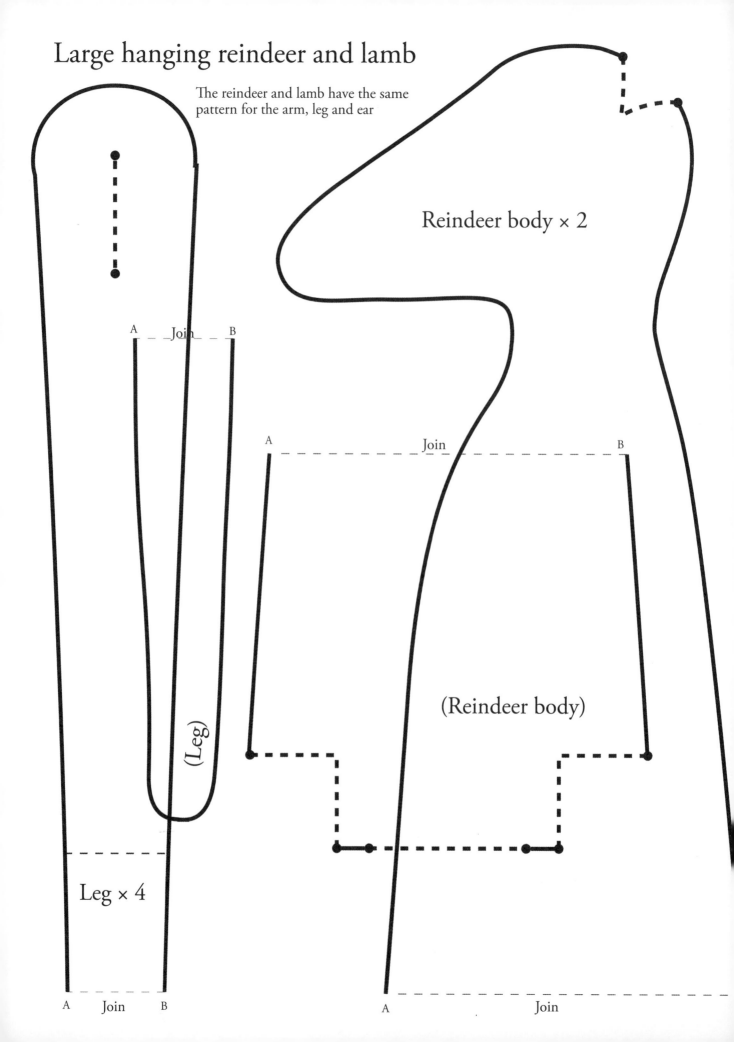

Reindeer body × 2

A — Join — B

A — Join — B

(Leg)

(Reindeer body)

Leg × 4

A   Join   B

A   Join

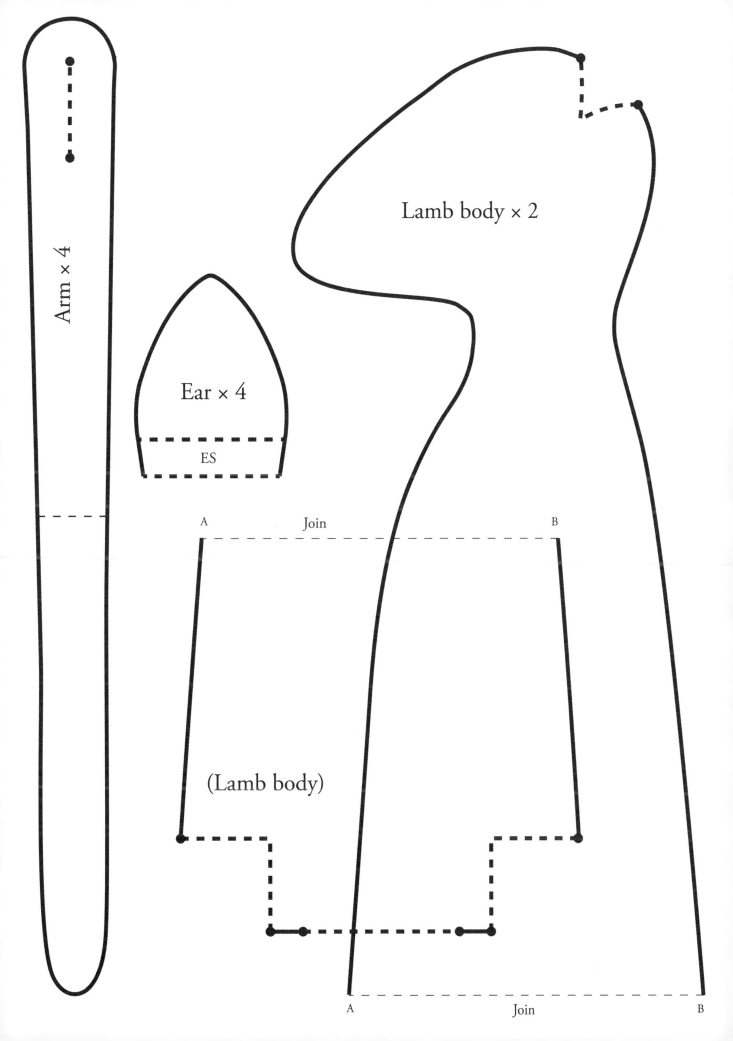

Arm × 4

Ear × 4

ES

Lamb body × 2

A

Join

B

(Lamb body)

A

Join

B

Christmas stocking: Birds in a tree

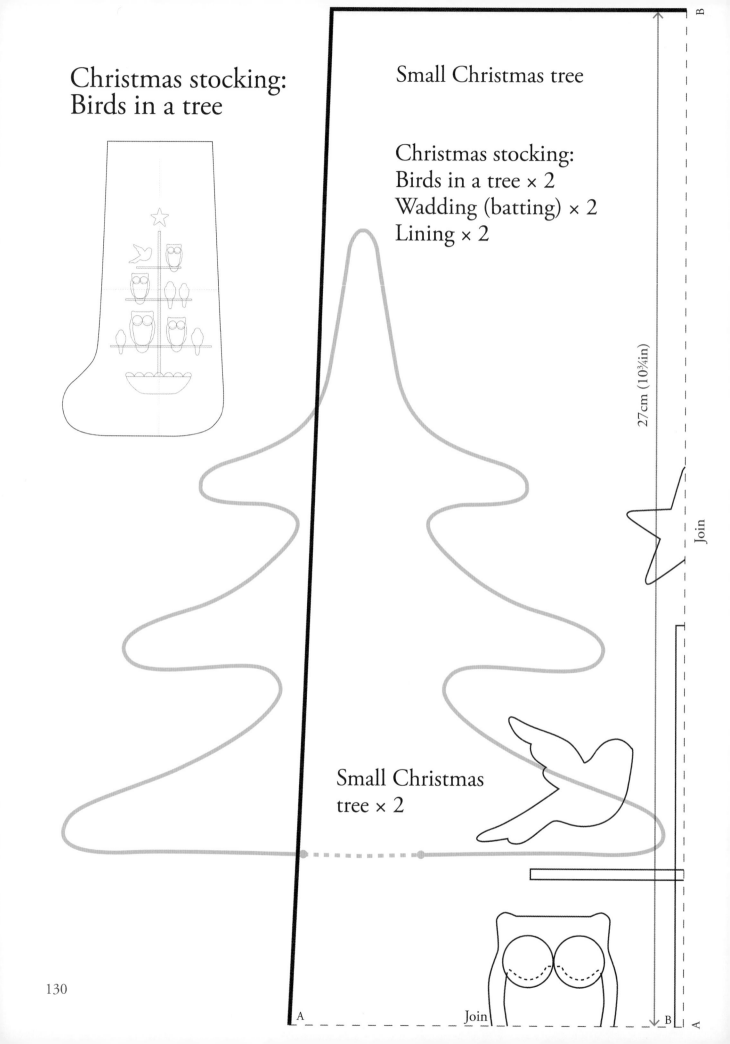

Small Christmas tree

Christmas stocking:
Birds in a tree × 2
Wadding (batting) × 2
Lining × 2

Small Christmas
tree × 2

27cm (10¾in)

Join

Join

A

B

B

A

130

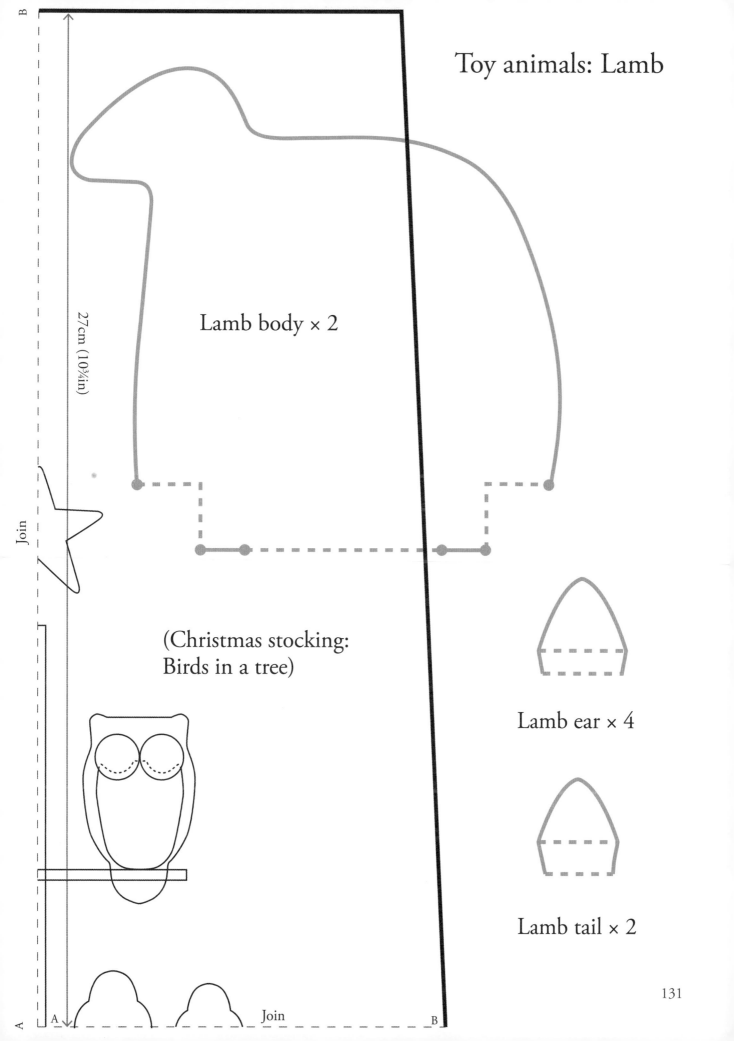

Toy animals: Lamb

Lamb body × 2

27cm (10¾in)

Join

(Christmas stocking:
Birds in a tree)

Lamb ear × 4

Lamb tail × 2

A

B

Join

B

131

Medium
Christmas
tree

(Christmas stocking:
Birds in a tree)

Medium
Christmas
tree × 2

26.5cm (10½in)

A

Join

B B

Join

A

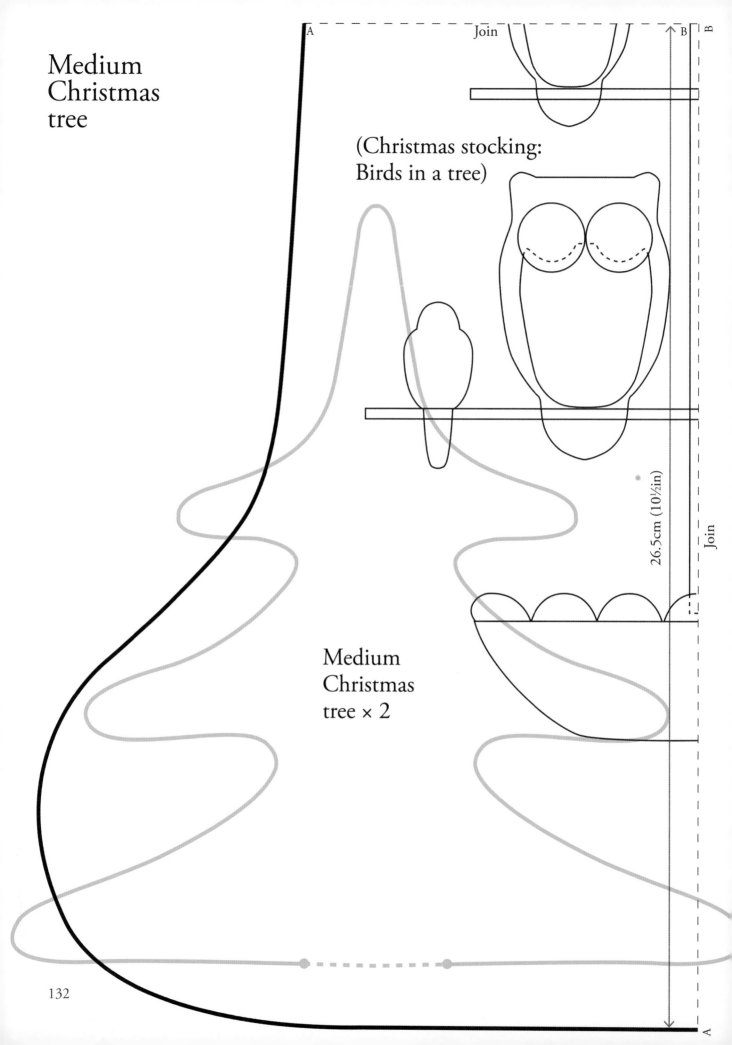

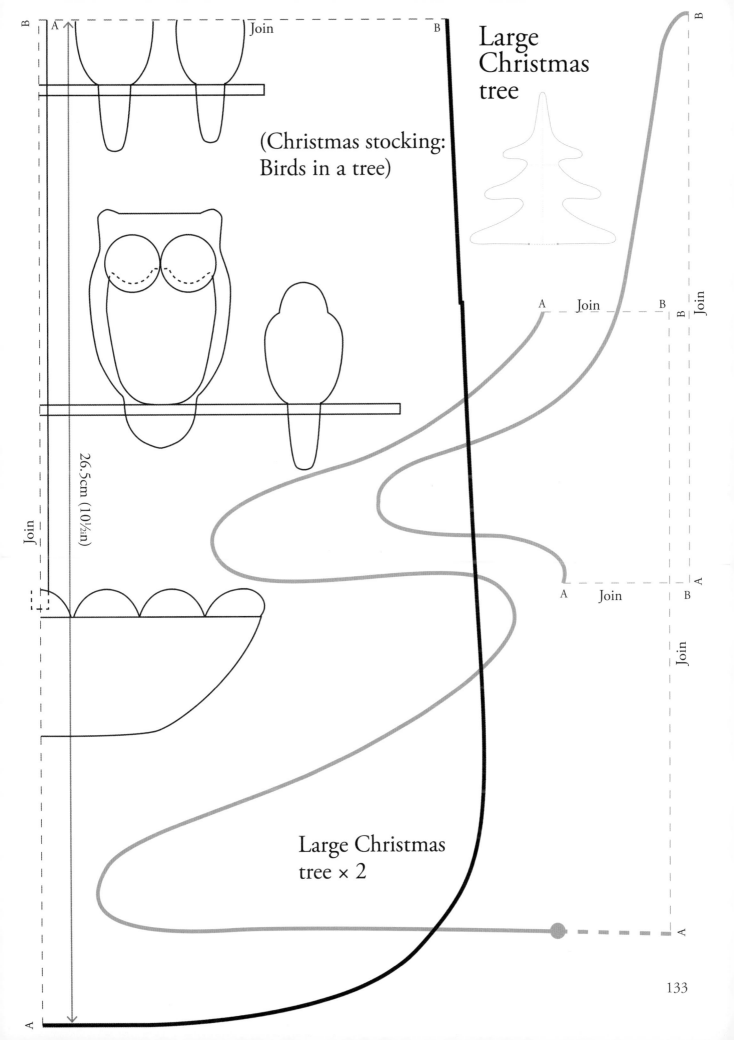

A   B   Join   B

(Christmas stocking:
Birds in a tree)

Large
Christmas
tree

26.5cm (10½in)

Join

Join

A   Join   B

A   Join   B
Join

A   Join   B

Large Christmas
tree × 2

A

Christmas stocking: Resting time

Reindeer and
lamb ear × 2

Christmas stocking
Resting time × 2
Wadding (batting) × 2
Lining × 2

27cm (10¾in)

Join

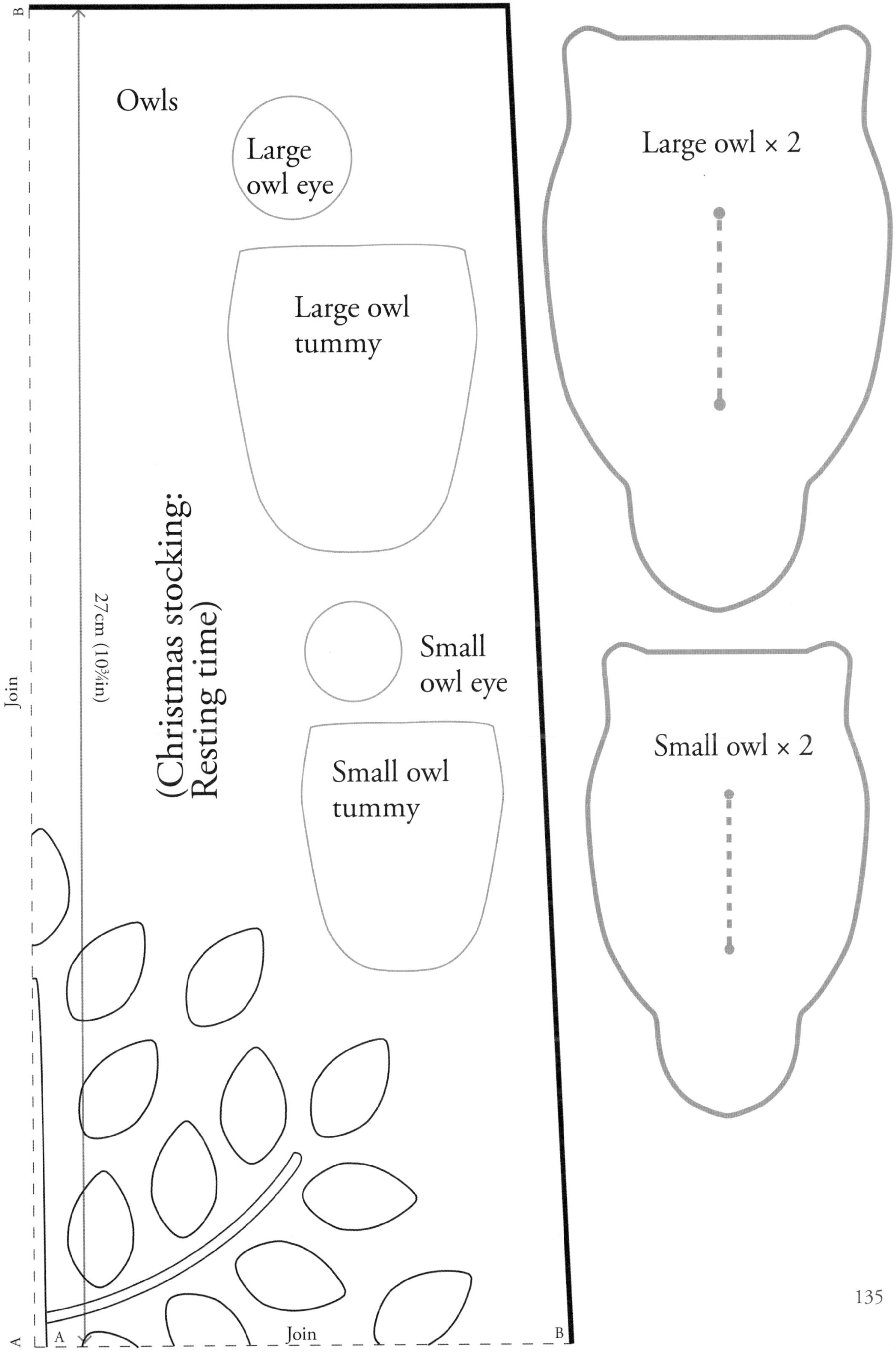

Owls

Large
owl eye

Large owl
tummy

Small
owl eye

Small owl
tummy

(Christmas stocking:
Resting time)

27cm (10¾in)

Join

A

B

A

Join

B

Large owl × 2

Small owl × 2

135

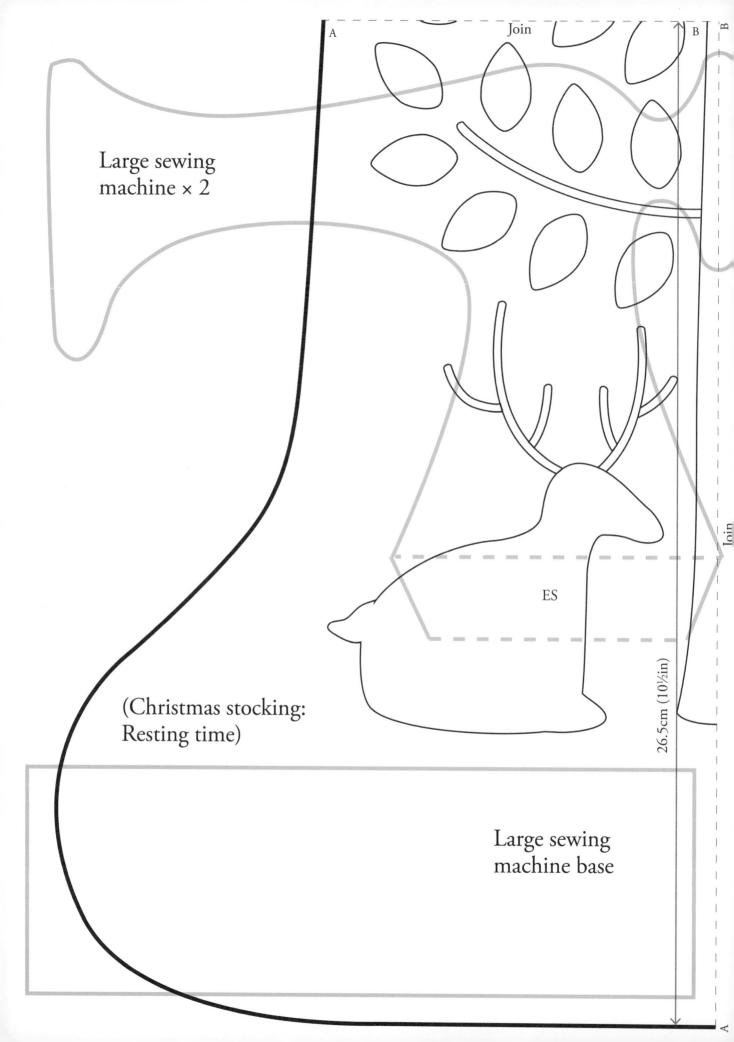

Large sewing
machine × 2

(Christmas stocking:
Resting time)

Large sewing
machine base

A

Join

B

B

Join

ES

26.5cm (10½in)

A

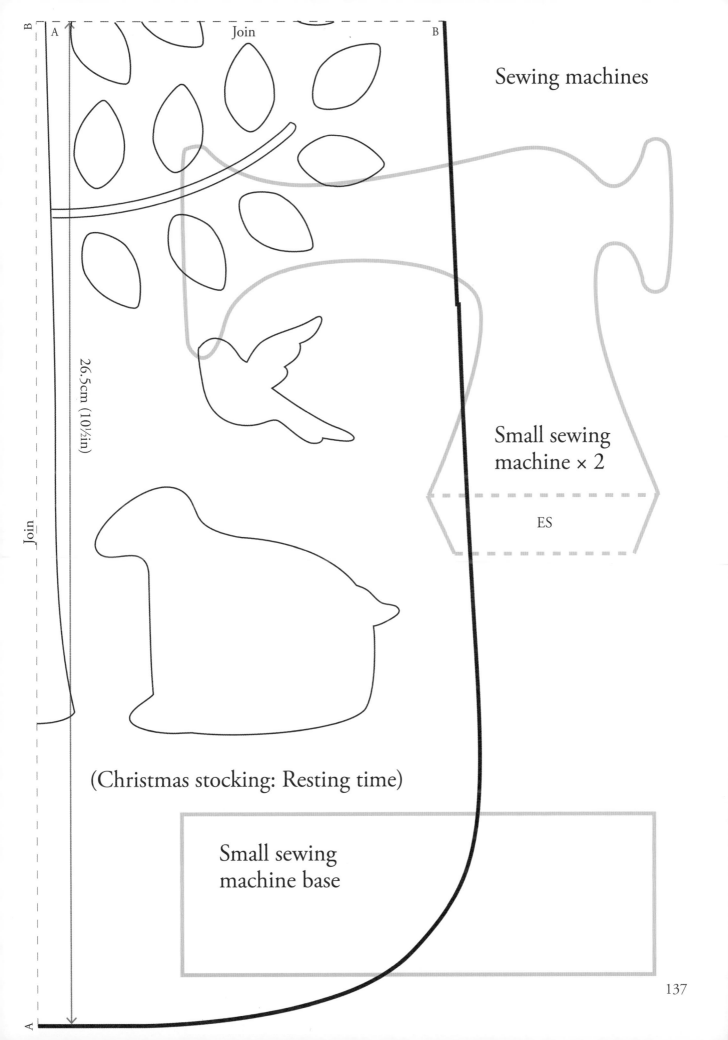

B A Join B

Sewing machines

26.5cm (10½in)

Small sewing
machine × 2

ES

Join

(Christmas stocking: Resting time)

Small sewing
machine base

A

A

137

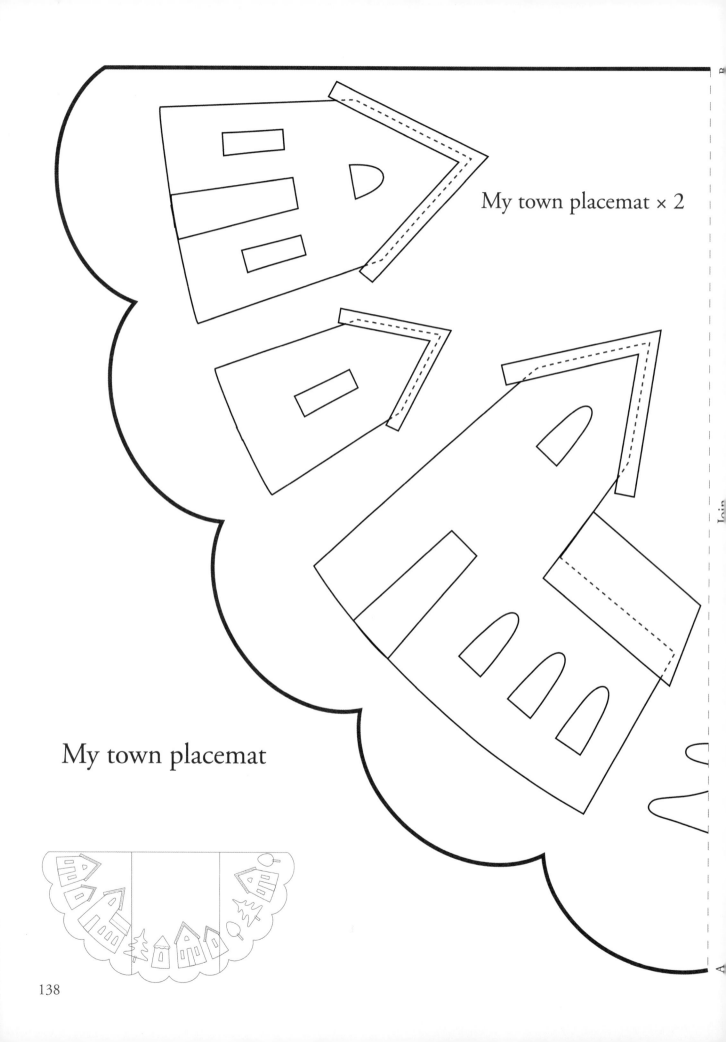

My town placemat × 2

My town placemat

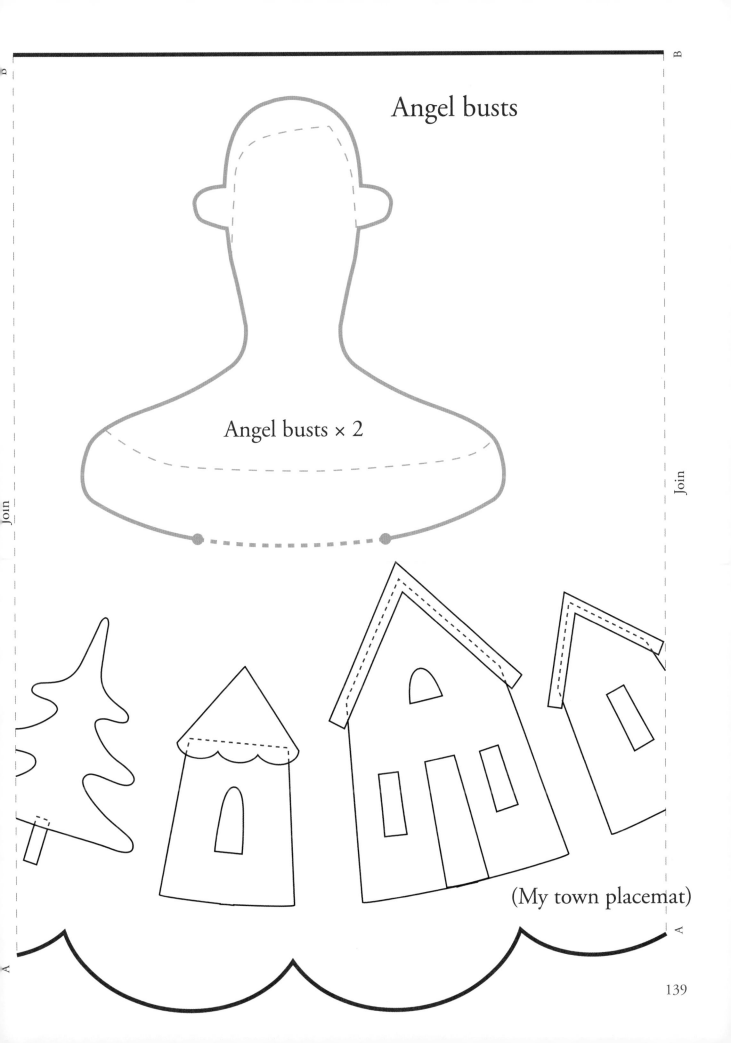

Angel busts

Angel busts × 2

(My town placemat)

Join

Join

A

A

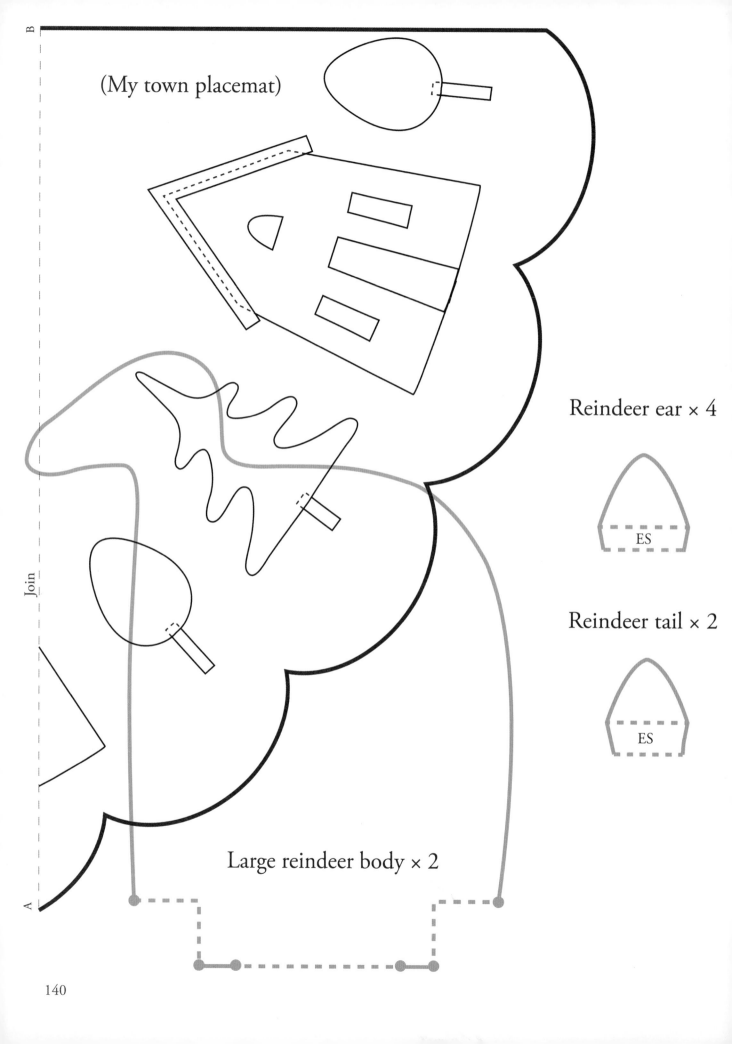

(My town placemat)

Reindeer ear × 4

ES

Reindeer tail × 2

ES

Join

Large reindeer body × 2

B

A

Purse

Toy animals: Reindeer

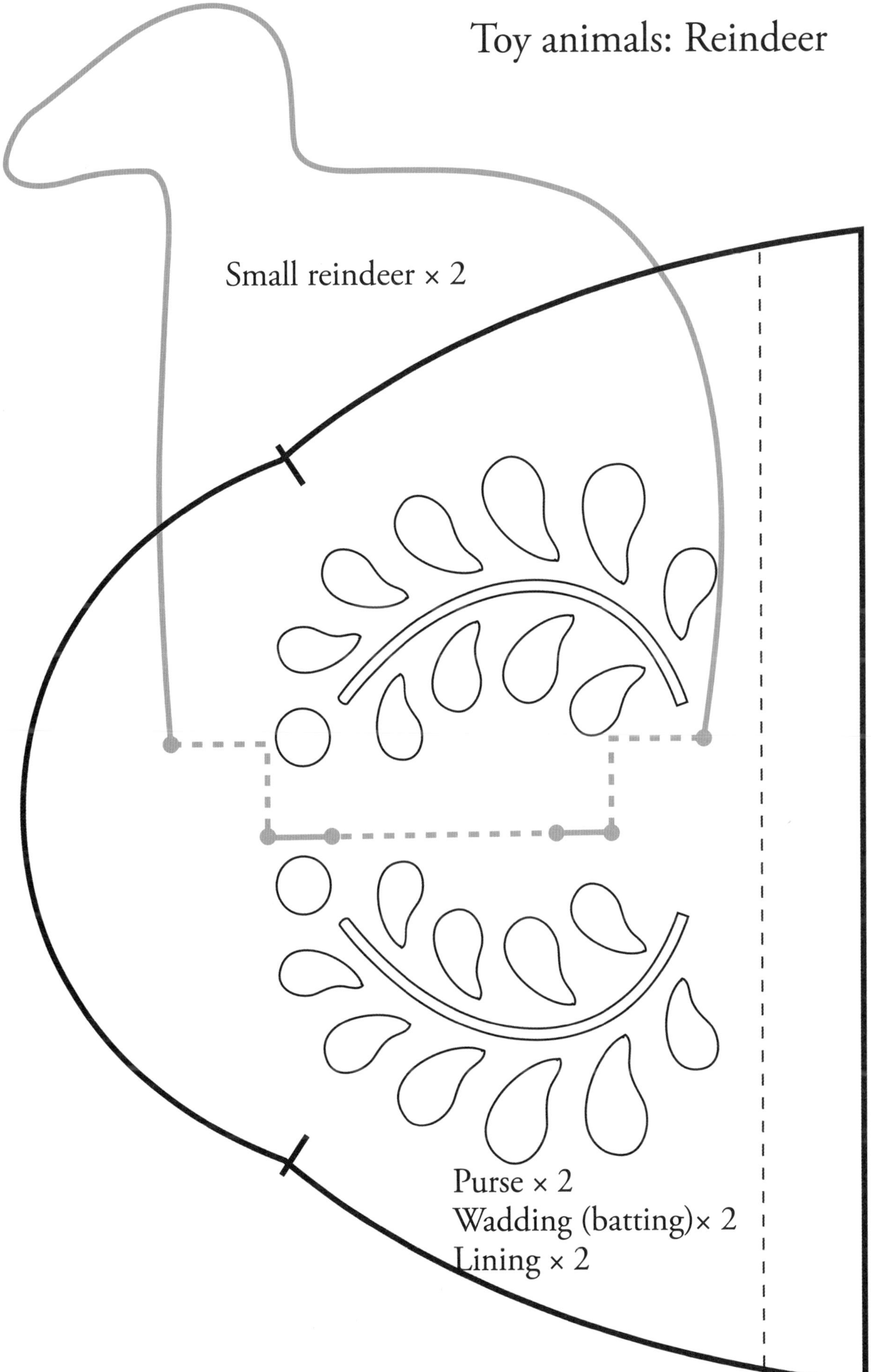

Small reindeer × 2

Purse × 2
Wadding (batting) × 2
Lining × 2

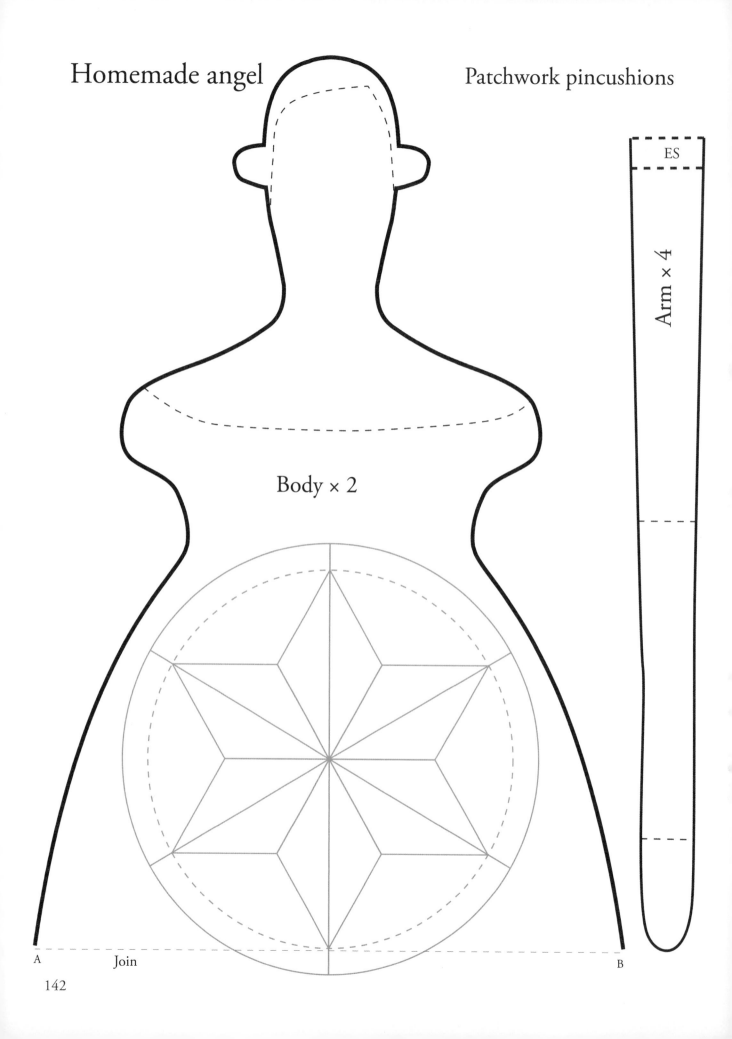

ES

Arm × 4

Body × 2

A

Join

B

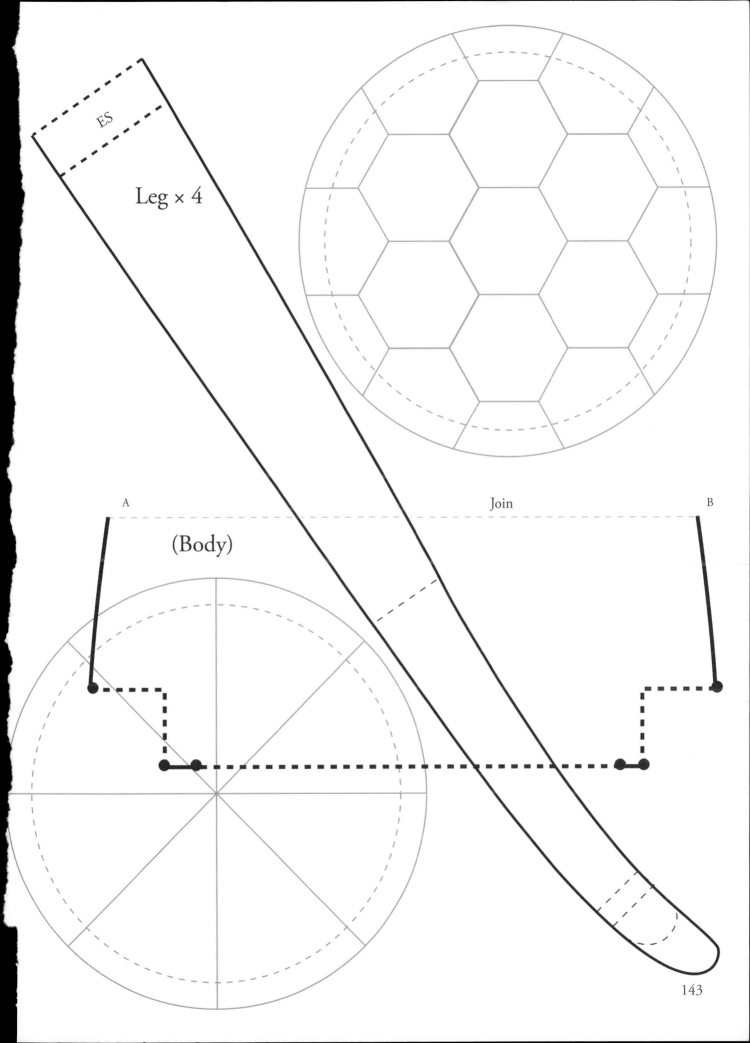

ES

Leg × 4

A   Join   B

(Body)

143

Index

A DAVID & CHARLES BOOK
© Cappelen Damm as 2014

Originally published in Norway as
Hjemmelaget og lykkelig
First published in the UK and USA in 2014 by
F&W Media International, Ltd

David & Charles is an imprint of F&W Media
International, Ltd
Pynes Hill Court, Pynes Hill, Exeter,
EX2 5AZ, UK

F&W Media International, Ltd is a subsidiary
of F+W Media, Inc
10151 Carver Road, Suite #200, Blue Ash,
OH 45242, USA

Tone Finnanger has asserted her right to be
identified as author of this work in accordance
with the Copyright, Designs and Patents Act,
1988.

The author and publisher have made every
effort to ensure that all the instructions in the
book are accurate and safe, and therefore
cannot accept liability for any resulting injury,
damage or loss to persons or property, however
it may arise.

Names of manufacturers and product ranges
are provided for the information of readers,
with no intention to infringe copyright or
trademarks.

A catalogue record for this book is available
from the British Library.

ISBN-13: 978-1-4463-0590-4 paperback
ISBN-10: 1-4463-0590-2 paperback

Printed in China by RR Donnelley
for F&W Media International, Ltd
Pynes Hill Court, Pynes Hill, Exeter,
EX2 5AZ, UK

15 14 13 12 11 10

Photographer: Sølvi Dos Santos
Stylist: Ingrid Skaansar
Illustrator: Tone Finnanger
Book design: Tone Finnanger

F+W Media publishes high quality books on a
wide range of subjects. For more great book
ideas visit: www.sewandso.co.uk